PLAYS BY RICHARD NELSON, EARLY PLAYS VOLUME ONE

BROADWAY PLAY PUBLISHING INC
56 E 81st St., NY NY 10028-0202
212 772-8334 fax: 212 772-8358
http://www.BroadwayPlayPubl.com

First printing: December 1998
ISBN: 0-88145-150-9

Book design: Marie Donovan
Word processing: Microsoft Word for Windows
Typographic controls: Xerox Ventura Publisher 2.0 PE
Typeface: Palatino
Copy-editing: Liam Brosnahan
Printed on recycled acid-free paper and bound in the USA

CONTENTS

PLAYS BY RICHARD NELSON

ACCIDENTAL DEATH OF AN ANARCHIST, *adaptation of Dario Fo*
AN AMERICAN COMEDY*
BAL*
BETWEEN EAST AND WEST*
CHESS, *libretto*
COLUMBUS AND THE DISCOVERY OF JAPAN
DON JUAN, *adaptation of Molière*
THE FATHER, *adaptation of Strindberg*
IL CAMPIELO, *adaptation of Carlo Goldoni*
THE GENERAL FROM AMERICA
GOODNIGHT CHILDREN EVERYWHERE
JITTERBUGGING: SCENES OF SEX IN A NEW SOCIETY*
LIFE SENTENCES
THE MARRIAGE OF FIGARO, *adaptation of Beaumarchais*
MISHA'S PARTY, *written with Alexander Gelman*
NEW ENGLAND
PRINCIPIA SCRIPTORIAE
THE RETURN OF PINOCCHIO*
RIP VAN WINKLE, OR "THE WORKS"*
ROOTS IN WATER*
SENSIBILITY AND SENSE
SOME AMERICANS ABROAD
THREE SISTERS, *adaptation of Anton Chekhov*
TWO SHAKESPEARIAN ACTORS
THE VIENNA NOTES*

**Published by Broadway Play Publishing Inc*

INTRODUCTION

Richard Nelson has gifts to spare. His talent, skill, wisdom, persistence and faith in the power of theater have led to an unprecedented American career. Irony, which infuses his writing, has come to inform his life. He is one of the most-produced American writers in Europe and England (particularly by the Royal Shakespeare Company), but Nelson's plays have enjoyed few major productions in the U S A. He writes passionately about his country's politics and morals, but his prime audiences are foreign. Nelson often creates plays built upon venomous characters and brutal scenes, but is himself generously loyal to family and colleagues. On stage and in life, there is no one quite like him. He inspires his friends, and I am one of them.

We've known each other since the summer of 1977. I was working then for the New York State Council of the Arts, and decided to check in on the Williamstown Theater Festival's Second Company, which had been given a grant to tour upstate New York communities. For some long-forgotten reason, I decided not to see the Second Company's production of A MIDSUMMER NIGHT'S DREAM, even though it was directed by an old college friend. Perhaps I'd been through too much Shakespeare that summer. I opted instead for the new play they were doing, Richard Nelson's CONJURING AN EVENT. I'd never heard of the author.

That Williamstown performance was the kind of theater-going adventure I've not had the luck to experience again: arriving at a theater with no expectations or awareness of the writer, and being enthralled—nailed to my seat—by completely unanticipated and inherently dramatic language. Here was a playwright of my own generation whose voice could cut through the hyperbole and fashion that irritate so much theatrical writing. This was talent, and a nice guy, too, as I discovered later that night over drinks. Since then, there have been countless drinks and dinners (in many states and countries) with Richard, his wife Cindy, and their children. I have been fortunate to work with Richard on two of his plays, and I am not alone among Richard's friends in having a deep-rooted need to be present wherever his latest work is staged. In the twenty-one years since CONJURING AN EVENT, I've missed a few Nelson openings in far-off cities—but not many.

This three-volume collection of Richard's early plays provides a welcome chance to revisit his exciting young work and the struggles of a writer's career. Work *and* career because Richard's ethics inform both and are inseparable. In the face of critical adversity towards these early plays that sometimes bordered on cruelty, Richard remained a prolific writer. There has hardly been a year when he has not had a new play ready for production. He never lost faith in his calling as a writer, displaying an almost spiritual strength in continuing his chosen work despite the brickbats. Important theater people matched that faith in championing Nelson on stage—most notably American producer Gregory Mosher, English director David Jones, and the Royal Shakespeare Company's literary manager Colin Chambers. Richard lost battles, but won wars.

The four plays in this first volume (THE KILLING OF YABLONSKI, CONJURING AN EVENT, JUNGLE COUP and the short monologue SCOOPING) were written between 1975 and 1977. An indication of the excitement sparked by Richard Nelson, whose plays first surfaced in informal workshops at the Mark Taper Forum in Los Angeles, is that the three full-length works included here were all produced by major not-for-profit New York theaters in back-to-back presentations between February and June 1978. It was a critical trial-by-fire, and a painful time for him, but these darkly comic plays have themes, character traits and theatrical set-ups that Nelson would refine in his acclaimed later work. The Chekhovian spirit that informs Nelson's mature plays is not yet evident, but many of the basic tenets of his writing are already in place.

From the start, Richard has been something of an American contrarian. In common with O'Neill, he often explores the dark side of American myth and bravado. The mid-1970s was the Post-Watergate era. Counter-culture investigative journalism brought down the Nixon White House, and reporters replaced rock stars as gods for the young. These four reporter plays aimed to burst the bubble of admiration that surrounded American journalism at that time.

When first staged, they seemed extreme to many audiences. How could a reporter conjure an event, create entirely fake stories about a revolutionary jungle coup, or confuse the reporting of an infamous murder with the egotistical act of scooping a lead? Today, the events in Richard's plays seem prescient. As I write this introduction, the Cable News Network and *Time* magazine have had to retract a lethal story about the use of nerve gas by American forces in Laos. In recent weeks, the *Boston Globe*, the *Cincinnatti Inquirer* and *The New Republic* have fired reporters, columnists, and editors for fabricating stories. The situations in Richard's reporter plays seemed extreme twenty years ago, but are plausible today. (In a weird twist of fate, the actor who played the self-absorbed reporter in the New York production of YABLONSKI, later became the host of a television talk show condemned for grunge exploitation and on-air scenes that were not that far from the imagined party games enjoyed by the family of Yablonski and their killers in Nelson's play.)

American blarney, extreme egotism, the confusion between humor and outrage, and the use of historical events to illuminate character are all techniques in the Nelson arsenal. These early plays show his abilities in different theatrical forms. The conciseness of SCOOPING, almost in echo of Beckett, gives hints of Nelson's later radio plays. JUNGLE COUP, which is a monologue for much of its length, evokes O'Neill's THE EMPEROR JONES, but shows Nelson's wonderful skill at narrative. The play is a simple situation that keeps turning on itself as two reporters invent ever-more outrageous stories for broadcast to their networks. We accept the exaggeration that the playwright builds and repeats because it becomes the heart of darkness for an enjoyably outrageous character.

As a hint of major Richard Nelson plays to come, THE KILLING OF YABLONSKI is perhaps the most interesting. The script has much Nelsonesque irony, as well as the Brechtian scene-titles he would use in many other works. The audience knows the Yablonski family's horrible real-life fate, but doesn't expect this brutal murder to become a reporter's fantasy in which his preposterous self-worth—not the loss of life—drives the narrative forward. The essence of the play is described not in its title, THE KILLING OF YABLONSKI, but in its subtitle: "Scenes of Involvement in a Current Event." The underbelly of personal involvement is what the playwright wants us to consider. The public event is not central, whether the established scene is the notorious Yablonski murder, New York's historic Astor Place Riot (TWO SHAKESPEAREAN ACTORS) or familiar New World legends (COLUMBUS AND THE DISCOVERY OF JAPAN). All these Nelson plays concern characters who make and use circumstances to their own ends, whether knowingly or blindly. The recognizable setting is just a stage convention.

Again, I come around to language, to Richard Nelson's exaggerated wordplays and riffs that first hooked me in CONJURING AN EVENT. Unlike his later, Chekhovian dramas, there's no underwriting in these early works. The words bounce off the stage with the driving energy of classic American comedy. Richard has a long-standing interest in American theater from the 1920s and 30s. The formative, staccato sound of newsroom reporters in THE FRONT PAGE (thickly filtered through a 1960s sensibility) infuses his early plays. But that's getting ahead of the game. Richard's love of 1930s American comedy is the story for another volume in this series.

Robert Marx is Executive Director of The New York Public Library for the Performing Arts.

CONJURING AN EVENT

CONJURING AN EVENT was first presented in workshop at The Mark
Taper Forum/Lab in 1976, directed by John Dennis, in a production
supported by the Office for Advanced Drama Research; and later presented
by The Williamstown Second Company, directed by Douglas C Wager.

CONJURING AN EVENT was produced by The American Place Theatre
(Wynn Handman, Artistic Director) on 15 March 1978. The cast and creative
contributors were:

CHARLIE . . . . Michael Cristofer
ANNABELLA . . . . Sigourney Weaver
SMITTY . . . . Dan Hedaya
WAITER . . . . John Jellison
MAN . . . . MacIntyre Dixon
SLEEVES . . . . Frank Hamilton

Director . . . . Douglas C Wager
Set designer . . . . David Lloyd Gropman
Costume designer . . . . William Ivey Long
Lighting designer . . . . Paul Gallo
Sound designer . . . . Carol Waaser

CHARACTERS

CHARLIE, *a reporter*
ANNABELLA, *his girlfriend*
SMITTY, *his older brother*
WAITER
MAN
SLEEVES, *a publisher*

ACT ONE

(Stage dark. Pause. Lights up on the Pen and Pencil Club. A large, heavy wooden table, large enough to seat eight, center left. On the table, candles, glasses, cups, etc, and a white lace tablecloth, which has been pushed away from stage right. Around the table, four or five straight leather chairs and a lamp or two between these chairs. Stage right, two or three high-backed comfortable chairs in a partial semicircle, facing down left. Next to the centermost chair, an end table. Upstage, a wooden newspaper rack. Everything very American Gothic. At the stage-right end of the table, CHARLIE (late twenties) sits. He wears a black eyepatch over each eye. His head is down so his face is nearly against the table. In front of CHARLIE, neatly layed out are a small china bowl, an ashtray, an empty china plate. ANNABELLA (CHARLIE's girl, mid-twenties) sits next to CHARLIE. She reads a couple of newsmagazines. Together at the far-left end of the table, SMITTY (CHARLIE's slightly older brother) sits, his focus on Mr SLEEVES, who is seated at the end of the table (facing right). SLEEVES, a publisher, is reading a manuscript, the pages of which are scattered on the table in front of him. In the centermost comfortable chair, a MAN (late thirties, athletic, though a shade overweight). He is reading a newspaper that is strung through a bamboo pole. He wears a turtleneck and slacks. Long pause as CHARLIE sniffs at the plate in front of him.)

CHARLIE: *(Yelling) Why can't I smell this!! (Suddenly, he grabs the plate, lifts it over his head, and smashes it against the edge of the table.)*

(SMITTY and SLEEVES do not look up. The MAN looks toward CHARLIE from over his paper. ANNABELLA continues to read. Pause. CHARLIE, trying to calm himself, speaks to himself.)

CHARLIE: Listen to the prep, Charlie. Listen to yourself. Is that what you want? Anger? Doubtful. It's times like this. As you prepare. Ready yourself to play all out to the finish. To dare. To go beyond. To rip up the margins. To pass the limits. The edges. To press unrestrained into absolute depth-reporting! It's times like this, Charlie. Pal. When you can't just fly off the handle. When you can't succumb. When you gotta press. Keep the effort intact. That initiative alive! The pressure on high, Charlie! Or else just figure yourself T K O'd on this score. Is that what you want, Charlie? Left to be like every other half-baked, part-time reporter who plays it safe with just facts and figures. Who plays his angle with no depth. No decent depth. Left covering tired stories. Beaten-to-death scoops. Doing a Woodward and Bernstein. A Reston and a Rather. Left with that sort of smoothy routine, Charlie. That sort of tired art form, full of cheap tricks, half efforts.

Bloodless! Lifeless, Charlie! No stakes involved. One-directional currents. Where the reporter sets up the rules so he can pull himself at any time. At will. Unplug. Unaffected by the tides. The heat. The pressures. The undertows. The whiplash. Where the reporter never dares to cross that line between himself and the story. Between the art and the artist. The drop and the ocean. Be like that, Charlie. Left doing that kind of number. You wanta stay stuck all your life doing that gritless-reporter routine? Too fuckin' scared to follow through? *You want that*? No you don't. 'Cause you see the hollowness in all that. The tricks. Fantasies. And lack of stamina in all that. You see past all that 'cause you've been there, Charlie. You've done your cover stories. Done your column with the personal flavor. You've exhibited your face. Your name. Your style. And voice. You've paraded your personal point of view! And now you are finished with all that! Washed your hands of all that! Now you are sick of all that! So now you are ready, Charlie. Ready to go beyond such natural observation. To move past the logic of those limits. That's the urge. To extend yourself and cover a story so close. Too close for comfort. Breathe down its neck. Closer than is possible. Natural. To dare! To prime the senses so as to touch, taste, smell it out. To flush it out! To become that pure, vacuous, senseful reporter. To compile beyond understanding. Faster than time. To wreck the boundaries of the senses. Timeless. Weightless. Selfless. A satellite! To pass through the Wolf, the Teddy White, the Cronkite, the Reasoner. To be on the inside, Charlie. The fuckin' inside! *The inside looking out!* Well, that's the urge, Charlie. The shape of the effort. The choice. Either pull out and run with the easy. The cheap and easy crowd. Or quit this crybaby stuff. This anger that's gonna crap up the movements. Quit it! And put your move back in motion. Let yourself go. And work at it, Charlie! You gotta work at it! And when you're polished, you'll know it. You'll be ready then. *(He puts his head back down against the table and begins to sniff the bowl. Pause)*

(ANNABELLA suddenly begins thumbing through her newsmagazine, back to front)

ANNABELLA: Still not a word, Charlie. Not a blessed word. I mean, it only makes sense! You'd think that with one of their own. When one of their kind attempts to. Dares. Well, after all, what we're doing is gonna affect them. It's gonna clear the way for them. Expand their scope. Their possibilities. Shit. You'd think they'd want to make it a big deal. Make a big splash out of this. I would. I certainly would if I were them.... Not a fuckin' comma.... *(She glances at the bowl CHARLIE is smelling.)* You picking anything up?

(CHARLIE doesn't answer.)

ANNABELLA: If not a headline, at least a mention in The Newsmakers. At least. But isn't that just the problem. With papers today. Wouldn't know a story if it bit 'em on the leg. Maybe we should just take the initiative, Charlie. Grab it. Point them in the right direction. Go after the

publicity. A touch of fame. Couldn't hurt, Charlie. A press conference. An interview.
To wet the imagination. Wire photos with captions: Reporter goes solo! Reporter goes all out: There's a story here. What the hell, it couldn't hurt! Maybe might even get us a grant or something. An angel, maybe....
(She checks out CHARLIE's *progress again.)* You want a hint?

CHARLIE: *No! (He takes deep sniffs.)* I ain't gettin' a decent beat on shit! How's my angle?

ANNABELLA: *(Checks out his position over the bowl)* You're right on top of it, Charlie. You're there, guy. Just go ahead and keep sniffing from there.

CHARLIE: *(Still over the bowl)* Oh sure. Great. Yeh. The way you mouth there's nothing to this number. *(He picks up his head.)* Wipe my forehead.

*(*ANNABELLA *wipes* CHARLIE's *forehead with a napkin.)*

CHARLIE: I'm just getting nothing I can take a good swing at. Nothing's clear. Clean. On the money. I'm being blocked. Blocked good! *Why the hell can't I sniff this!*

ANNABELLA: Take your time, guy. Take it slow. The smells will come.

CHARLIE: *(Waving her back)* All right. All right. Stand back. I'll keep the heat on. I'll keep swinging through. You back?

ANNABELLA: *(She leans away from* CHARLIE.) Yeh.

(Pause. CHARLIE *begins to smell again. Harder.* ANNABELLA *returns to her magazines.)*

ANNABELLA: Maybe if we gave them a nudge. In our direction. A lead-in. Put them on the right track. After all, they can't exactly deny that they've got the space. Anyone could see they do. Anyone with eyes. Half this goddamn sheet is pumped with fillers. Shaggy dog stories. Replays. You'd think they'd be eager. Beat a path to our door. Do a Man in the News bio. You'd think, wouldn't you? It only makes sense. A mention. Not one damn mention. What the hell are they afraid of?

CHARLIE: *(Sniffing very hard now)* Hey. Wait a sec! Wait a sec! I'm getting something now. I am. I am. I'm tuning in. It's passing through. The smell. This. Feel it. Feel it. Something's coming through.

ANNABELLA: *(She sets her magazines down; tense, excited)* Is it, Charlie? You sure?

CHARLIE: Shut up. *(He sniffs even harder.)* Yes. Yes. Define. Crystallize. Sharpen. It's a.... It's a.... it's a common smell....

ANNABELLA: *(She bends over to look in the bowl.)* That's correct, guy.

CHARLIE: Hardly a day goes by without ya getting a whiff of this smell. Am I right?

ANNABELLA: Yes! Yes, you're absolutely right.

CHARLIE: And this smell...it's of...I'm pinpointing. Plotting. It's of....
I'm on the track. Boy, does this feel great. Of...of...of...

ANNABELLA: Of what? What?

CHARLIE: (*Triumphant. He picks up his head.*) Paper!! It's paper! That's it.
I'm smelling paper. No doubt about it. No static. Clear as a bell. Paper!
(*He returns to smelling.*) That...that low-grade stuff. Made half out of rag.
Rag bond. Wrinkled. Creased. But recently pressed.

ANNABELLA: (*Calm again*) Smell again, guy. I think you must have caught a
crosswind from somewhere else.

CHARLIE: I said, it's paper!

ANNABELLA: (*She picks up her magazine again.*) Give it another run, guy.
Go ahead.

CHARLIE: It's not paper? But I'm positive. It's perfectly clear to me. I swear....
I must at least be close. (*He gives it another big sniff.*)

(WAITER *enters near* MAN. *He carries a couple more bamboo poles with newspapers
strung through.*)

WAITER: Another paper, sir?

(MAN *ignores him.* MAN *stares at* CHARLIE. WAITER *exits.*)

CHARLIE: (*Giving up*) Okay. What the hell is it then?

ANNABELLA: It's salt, Charlie.

CHARLIE: Salt? Are you kidding? You for real? That should be an easy move.
....I'm smelling paper!

ANNABELLA: I'll go back to the kitchen and get some fresh smells.
Don't worry, guy. You're gonna turn this trick. You'll do it. (*She exits.*)

MAN: Waiter!

CHARLIE: Yeh. Do it. Just do it. Shit.... Salt? I'm smelling paper!
(*He continues to sniff.*)

(WAITER *enters.*)

WAITER: (*To* MAN) A paper, sir?

MAN: Does this club stock any New York State wine?

WAITER: Yes, sir. We carry...

MAN: Great Western Chablis, by any chance? (*He pronounces the "s".*)

WAITER: I believe. Yes, I'm sure that we do carry....

MAN: Then be a good sport, and take a bottle over to that gentleman there. *(He nods toward* CHARLIE.*)*

WAITER: That gentleman? Yes, sir. *(He exits.)*

(Short pause)

*(*SLEEVES *sighs and puts down the manuscript.* SMITTY, *who has been closely watching* SLEEVES *as he read, now anxiously waits for his reaction.)*

SMITTY: *(Finally:)* Well?

SLEEVES: *(In a fog)* Well what?

SMITTY: What do you think, Mr Sleeves? Ain't that got juice?

*(*SLEEVES *doesn't respond.)*

SMITTY: Charlie's book, Mr Sleeves. Don't it pack enough wallop to knock you on your ass? My brother's a real genius for reporting a story. Ain't he....? Mr Sleeves....? You there? It's spellbinding stuff. It'll catch the Public Eye. Dead center. Well...

SLEEVES: *(He sighs again, looks around.)* Jeeze, it's nice being back with reporters again. Nice. This club. Feel the journalistic beat. Rhythm. Magic. Can't say I haven't missed it.

SMITTY: *(Confused)* Oh, sure. Yeh....But I ain't no reporter, Mr Sleeves. That's Charlie's trick. I'm just peddling his book here—

SLEEVES: *(He does not really hear him.)* I know. I know that....I was a reporter, Smitty. Once. Way the hell back. Before your time. Before almost everybody's time now. Before TV. Satellites. Synthetic grass and domed stadiums. A whole different kind of ballgame back then. You wouldn't know the rules. Energy. Electricity. Magic. Art—back then. You felt it on the back of your neck. Hair sticking up. Understand?

SMITTY: Heck no!

SLEEVES: Maybe you do. Maybe you do. Ever hear of the Algonquin Group?

SMITTY: The what?

SLEEVES: That was a roundtable club—actually twelve square tables pushed together in the hotel's dining room. But it looked almost round when we were done. That was in New York. ....Talk. Talk. Talk. Drink. That kind of club.

SMITTY: Yeh. That kind of club. Sure. But, Mr Sleeves. About the book...

SLEEVES: Ben Hecht. Ring Lardner. Marc Connelly. Charlie McArthur. Dorothy Parker. I could go on. More names. The tops. The greats. Hall of fame. Muscle. At our peak almost thirty of us—combining more raw knowledge of the way the world turned than any thousand jokers alive. We were reporters. With a capital R. If you know what I mean.

SMITTY: I don't!

SLEEVES: We'd sit and shoot the bull. Handicap politicians in an election. Exchange recent scoops. Except on the nights when one of us would get a call, a tip on a fast news break. A mug who'd been shot up. A world leader who'd snuck into our town for an operation or 'a little on the side.' If you know what I mean. Just one phone allowed. So everyone could hear. That was the rule. Then all thirty of us would tear out, upsetting tables, chairs, the buxom barmaid, slug down a last whisky, and run for daylight and the morning editions. Front page! Hold the front page: I got a scoop: Yes. Magic. *(Short pause)*

SMITTY: Mind if I smoke? *(He lights a cigarette.)*

SLEEVES: There was an energy. A reporter felt like an artist. He had somethin' driving him on. No, it weren't money then. Or broads. Or your name in caps. It was electricity. You was on your belly, eye to eye with the earth. Watch it spin. Clock its time. Energy. Touching the live wires. Feel the heat. Near. Close. Pulse. Pulse. Our experiences were poems. They'd move folks to tears, laughter. Hair sticking up. Papers were read then. Meant something. A lot. Everything almost. So you'd feel the muscle, getting men and women choked up, their guts strung tight. And the magic. Cause we didn't understand any better than the ordinary Joe on the street did. How it happened. But we felt it better. Magic. And muscle. *(Pause)* And that's when it happened. I can't forget. I'm sorry. The magic was most potent too. That's when the telegrams came. Money. We want you. We all got wires from Babel. Our name for Hollywood. Jaded City. Like a faucet had been turned on, the energy, it just flowed away. To get diluted. Gummed up. Offers of five hundred bucks a week to write for the talkies when we was making that in three months. So. We push together only five tables at first. Then three. Finally one square table was all we needed. MacArthur. Hecht. Lardner. Connelly. Parker. I could go on. All gone. Gone away. Goodbye. I tried. So hard. Gritted my teeth. Bit my lip. Held the line. Keep the art alive. The magic. Keep the ball. Talk about swimming pools. How they don't like snow no more. It was gone. Goodbye. The magic fades fast when it's diluted. I don't regret staying. I don't. I tried.

(Long pause. The WAITER *enters with the wine. He sets it on the table in front of* CHARLIE. *No one pays any attention to him. He exits.)*

SLEEVES: *(He abruptly changes his tone.)* Well. We were talking about this manuscript, weren't we, Smitty?

SMITTY: Charlie's manuscript? This one here? You wanta talk about? Well, I'll be. Well, I'll be damned. I thought I'd gone and lost you for good back there.

SLEEVES: *(Ignoring* SMITTY*)* As I was saying, Smitty...

SMITTY: Saying? You weren't saying nothin' I could make sense out of, Mr Sleeves.

SLEEVES: *(He pats the manuscript.)* What this book needs...is a bit more punch, Smitty. More...pizazz. Flash.

SMITTY: Flash?

SLEEVES: Right now, it's awfully raw stuff. It's good. Maybe great. Who knows for sure? Who can ever be positive? But it's raw. Raw. There's a heck of a lot of work still to be done on this, Smitty. It's gonna have to be cooked quite a bit.

SMITTY: Well, if that's all that's troubling you. Sure. I mean we know that. Don't we Charlie? It's just a mass of articles now, but Charlie, he'll whip it into shape with no sweat.

SLEEVES: It's all...muscle. In fact, one might say it's pure muscle. And what muscle at that. And that's good, Smitty. A plus. Powerful. Quite exceptional, really. Electricity! It's hot. You can just feel it. Feel it.

(SMITTY puts his hand on the manuscript.)

SLEEVES: But where are the bones, Smitty? There aren't any bones to hang all that muscle on: The bones, Smitty. Do you feel any?

SMITTY: No. I guess I don't. No bones.

SLEEVES: But I can do that myself. Construct the bones. *(He turns to another page.)*

SMITTY: You? Construct the bones? Wait a minute. What I miss? Are you hinting that you're interested in doing the book, Mr Sleeves?

SLEEVES: You know, Smitty, this story here, this...event.

SMITTY: Yeh. 'Course I know it. I read the book. You keep jumping around from one thing to somethin different. How 'bout holding one note for a while. O K, Mr Sleeves? Now let me see if I can get this straight. Are you interested or what in publishin' Charlie's book?

SLEEVES: I was saying to myself, at the time this story broke. I was saying what a Jim Dandy book it could make. Isn't that amazing, Smitty? Really quite remarkable.

SMITTY: Was that a yes or a no?

SLEEVES: Just for starters, Smitty. So you can see what all has to be done. The time involved. The effort. Work. Sweat. With something like this. In fiddling with the movement. Tightening the strings. Quickening the pulse. Pulse. Just for starters, let's take this title. In fact, go ahead and take it. 'Cause it's all wrong. Might even say, it's bad. No angle. No bite. No zing. You need an angle to grab guts with, Smitty. Guts. To make a big splash!

SMITTY: Yeh. A splash. Right. Uh, you know, Mr Sleeves, I ain't got much of a grip on what you've been saying. Now that ain't necessarily your fault. But maybe if ya spoke with Charlie. I mean, he's right at home with the artistic talk. *(He turns to* CHARLIE, *waving him over; in a loud whisper:)* Charlie!

SLEEVES: But I'll come up with something, Smitty. Don't you worry. Always did, didn't I? Before. Way the hell back. Started off my career writing headlines for the obits. If that didn't tax the imagination, nothing could.

SMITTY: Yeh, I guess so. *(To* CHARLIE; *whisper)* Charlie! Quick, guy. Quick! I think he's interested. I think he might do it. Charlie! Come on, guy, come on. Did you hear what I said. He might do it.

SLEEVES: Just give me time. To roll up my sleeves. Plunge in. Get used to the currents. Get back the touch. The feel. I had it once. I did. Before. What a touch.

SMITTY: Sure, what's the rush. No sweat. *(To* CHARLIE*)* What the hell's wrong with you? Charlie, will you pay attention. Jesus Christ. Charlie!

SLEEVES: *(Yells) Just give me time!* I'll come up with something big. Juicy. It'll come to me. In a rush. Like before. I'll just be standing somewhere, having a sandwich, thinking about something else and it'll come. Something to make people take notice. Give 'em a chill. Hair sticking up. Give me time: I'll do it! *I'll do it!*

SMITTY: *(Now more confused by this outburst)* Uh. Sure. Easy there, Mr Sleeves. Just take it slow. Take your time. What's the hurry. I mean, no big rush, is there? *(Loud voice)* Charlie! Will you pay attention: Will you quit that stupid smelling and listen!

SLEEVES: *(He suddenly looks up at* SMITTY. *Cold. Direct)* What did you say?

SMITTY: Huh?

SLEEVES: What the fuck did you say!!

SMITTY: Me? I told Charlie to stop his smelling and pay attention. I mean, he should know what's going on. It's his book.

SLEEVES: Is that what he's doing? Smelling? I thought he was drunk.

SMITTY: I guess he sort of looks that way, don't he?

SLEEVES: Why is he smelling, Smitty?

SMITTY: It ain't that important, Mr Sleeves.

SLEEVES: It's important to me!

SMITTY: Well, Charlie, he could explain it a lot better than me, but, see, he says he's sharpening his sense of smell. To prepare himself...uh. He's sort of worked out that smelling is the way in. See A clue. A secret. Least that's what he says.

SLEEVES: A way in? I'm not sure I follow.

SMITTY: I don't either really, Mr Sleeves. It's just some crazy notion Charlie's got that after covering events live, you know, first-hand, like this book here. After reporting for so long. Then the next step, he says, well, it's to learn to conjure...to conjure a story up...an event up. I think it's some artistic binge. A fad, you know. Won't come to nothin'. But that's what he's preparing for. That's why he's smelling.

SLEEVES: *(He has turned pale and begun to shake.)* Conjure an event?

SMITTY: Yeh. Pretty crazy, huh?

SLEEVES: *(Jumping out of his seat, he screams.)* Don't let him do it! Stop him! Stop him! *(Panicking,* SLEEVES *runs out. Upset. Scared shitless. Short pause)*

SMITTY: Mr Sleeves? Mr Sleeves! What the hell got into you? What about the book? The book. *(He runs out after him.)*

(Pause. CHARLIE *picks up his head.)*

CHARLIE: Christ, what a racket'. Can't hear myself think. How's a Joe supposed to get any work done with all this shoutin' going on? Shit. No wonder I'm getting nowhere fast. Pissing in my pants. Them talking on my backswing. Drowning out my signals. Breaking down my rhythm. So's I can't sustain the drive! *No peace and quiet! (Deep breath)* Yeh. I'm perfecting my sense of smell. Number-one move. Smelling is the way into a conjure all right. To prime the senses. Numero-uno step. To ready the tools needed to make that big break. Necessary to gain the inside. To lessen the friction. *But I got too many goddamn interruptions! (Short pause.* CHARLIE *continues to sniff. Then looks up)* Wait a sec. Wait a sec. Now who am I kidding? Huh? Just who am I hustling this round? I'm pulling on my own fucking leg. Blaming bad play on a bit of chatter. That's sour-grape-itis, man. You are losing. Losing bad. And you're grabbing at excuses. Cheap. Cheap and easy. Hunting for a chance to blunt your own damn urge, Charlie! That ain't like you. Ain't your number. You know better than that. You're no Weiskopf. You're no Nastase. Find no alibi in a bad call. Ain't gonna quit over the condition of the course. Not you, guy. Not your angle. *(Short pause. Deep breath)* This kind of stroke, well it's just gonna take time. Patience. Patience. It ain't easy. You knew that before ya started. To attempt. To break out. Knew you'd be swinging on a thread. Dancing on a blade. It'll just take time. Time. Pace. My edge—gotta be razor sharp. My timing—right on. My speed—fast. My reflexes—a whip. It'll come, guy. All that will come. I'll pull this score off, all right. In time. No sweat. I've cracked hard scores before. Though nothin quite like this. On this scale. Well, just do it: Yeh. Head down. Feet set. Solid concentration. Focus. Good balance. Hang tough. Hang in there. Action. Now, give it a big sniff. Do it! Do it! *(He sniffs harder. Harder. Looks up)* Crap! Just do it? Just do it? That's easier said, guy. Easier flashed than put into play. Yeh. *Why can't I smell out salt!*... An easy move. Beginner stuff. Slow ball. Snap, and I should have it. But I smell ten things at once and can't pick out the right one! I'm groping when I should be absorbing. I'm reacting when I should be on top! I keep coming up empty. Called out looking! I'm still knocking at the goddamn door! I've got the desire. I've wanted this. Wanted this bad. I've put my time in. Haven't I? I'm practicing. I've practiced. So where's it got me? How far? How deep? Me. Me. Got me! Nothing. Nowhere. Trying. Coming up empty-handed. I am spent, I tell you! Complete! That's enough! I've had enough! I've had enough! *(He picks up the salt bowl, holds it for a second over his head and then smashes it against the floor. He begins to stare down at the table.)*

(Pause. The MAN *has been watching and listening to* CHARLIE. *He now takes out a pile of red three-by-five file cards, shuffles them, then begins writing on them— still with one eye on* CHARLIE. *He writes throughout the remainder of the act.)*

*(*ANNABELLA *enters with a tray of food—smells—covered by a white cloth.)*

ANNABELLA: I've got more smells from the kitchen, Charlie. Where's Smitty?

CHARLIE: I don't know. He was yelling somethin' and I think he run off.

ANNABELLA: With that publisher guy?

CHARLIE: I don't know. I was busy. Didn't pay no attention.

ANNABELLA: I brought you more smells.

CHARLIE: Don't bother no more 'bout that. I'm gonna take a break for a while.

ANNABELLA: Sure, Charlie. It must be kinda tough work.... I'll put them on the table. *(She does)*

CHARLIE: I'm feelin' a little lightweight. Suspended. Out of it. I need some rest.

ANNABELLA: You just say when, guy, and I'll set you up to try another smell.

CHARLIE: I mean, I'm gonna take a long break.... Like maybe a month or two. I wanta recharge myself, get my feet on the ground again, and come back to this run fresh. I'm feeling stale. Maybe I pushed myself too hard these past two weeks.

ANNABELLA: *(Confused)* A month?

CHARLIE: Yeh. Maybe two. Or three. Or four. Who the hell knows? Long as it takes to get my head back in working shape.

ANNABELLA: Four months? Hey, guy... I never heard you talk about having to recharge yourself before. You always said you got a lot of good feedback *from* your work.

CHARLIE: Well, sure. Sure. Yeh, I do.... I mean, I used to, see. But this is different, okay? Real different. Another kind of ballgame completely. Look, this conjuring route ain't in stages like my other stuff, where I could move in or out at will, take a break when the mood struck, keep as big a distance between me and the show as I wanted. Here the force has got to come from you. Only from you, see. It's total involvement, see.

ANNABELLA: Sure, Charlie.

CHARLIE: So it's dangerous. Yeh. It's either win or lose. Success/failure. So's it can burn you out quick. Zap! No chance to gather momentum. Keep your bearings. You either hit the jackpot or you wear yourself out trying. *And I am wearing myself out good!*

ANNABELLA: Hey guy...?

CHARLIE: Damn it, *I just need to unplug for a while!!*

(Short pause)

ANNABELLA: Guy...? Are you pulling out?

CHARLIE: *(Quick; very defensive)* Is that what you think?

ANNABELLA: It' s just—*four months*, Charlie.

CHARLIE: *Is that what you think?!!! Is it?!!* Shit. Well, if it is. If it...then maybe. Well, maybe you just oughta start slinking yourself out of here. Out of earshot. Real fast. Real fast. Yeh. Well, maybe you oughta just stop mumbling under your breath. Mumbling, "Poor Charlie. He don't know what the fuck he's doing. Too bad what's happening to Charlie."

ANNABELLA: I ain't been mumbling nothing, Charlie.

CHARLIE: Stop mumbling, yeh, and maybe start telling me, "Hey, Charlie. Hey there. I'll be right back in a sec. Just gotta run off around the corner." *And then start running!! And keep running!! So run!! Run!!! Come on, damn it. Run!!! (Pause. He covers his head.)*

ANNABELLA: *(Depressed because she figures* CHARLIE'*s effort to conjure is over; but she tries to hide her depression.)* Hey, guy, you know, I'm feelin pretty edgy myself.... I mean, what the hell, right? What the fuck, a break couldn't hurt, could it?

*(*CHARLIE *doesn't respond.)*

ANNABELLA: I mean, what we've already got going, we ain't gonna lose by pausing for a few beats, right? In fact, might do a whole lot of good. As you say, Charlie, we could come back feeling fresh. Come back feeling on our toes again. Get the rhythm back in the bounce, right? The strength in the grip, right?

*(*CHARLIE *remains turned away.* ANNABELLA *wants his attention.)*

ANNABELLA: I didn't mean you was really pulling out, guy. I didn't mean that at all. *(Short pause)* Hey, Charlie, what about the World Series. That's comin' up, right? How about hittin' that and turning a sports reporter trick? You know, just for the fun of it. Just to get the juices free again. There's no pressure in that. The format's easy. And, shit, they always got free beer and sandwiches in the press room. What do you say? (*No response*) Yeh, just like we used to, guy. You know? Like in St Petersburg. You remember St Petersburg, don't you?

(CHARLIE *remains turned away.*)

ANNABELLA: Hey, what *was* that system you had going down there? Remember?

(*No response, though he is relaxing a bit*)

ANNABELLA: At night.... Let me see if I've got this right. At night, you worked in the press department at the Wrestling Arena. Am I right? You were writing releases for the two local dailies. Was that it? (*Short pause*)

CHARLIE: Yeh.

ANNABELLA: And then in the morning...right? Under a different name, you did sports for the afternoon paper. Rewriting your own press releases. Right? And there was something else, wasn't there?

CHARLIE: In the afternoon, under still another name—

ANNABELLA: You rewrote your releases again for the morning paper! *Right!*

(CHARLIE *looks up.*)

ANNABELLA: Shit, you had yourself a monopoly going, didn't you? Total control. You caught the news coming and going.

CHARLIE: I ran the whole fucking show.

(*Short pause*)

ANNABELLA: Yeh, that was a whole lot of fun. Just working in low gear. Just trottin' around the bases. They were great times. Weren't they?

CHARLIE: Wait a sec. Wait one sec. And what was it you were doing down there? I remember you was into somethin' pretty smooth down there too.

ANNABELLA: Yeh, I was doing a kid journalism number, Charlie. Kid journalism. News for kids.

CHARLIE: Yeh, that's right.

ANNABELLA: *Weekly Reader* stuff. I rewrote the news so kids could read it. Change the few big words. Pick stories kids might like. That kind of setup.

CHARLIE: (*Smiling*) I remember.

ANNABELLA: Great times. They were. No danger. For either of us. The forms were easy. We had the outline. And we were just filling it in.... We were sittin' pretty. And we were happy, weren't we, guy?

(Short pause)

CHARLIE: *(Suddenly explodes) God damn it!!!!!* Shit, why 'dyou bring up that for? You tryin' to subvert me? Is that it?!! *Is that it?!*

ANNABELLA: What are you talking about?

CHARLIE: Make me take a nice high dive into the past?

ANNABELLA: What???

CHARLIE: *Well, damn it!! Damn it!!! I ain't built for that! I ain't built for that!! I am a reporter, not no god damn historian!!!!!!*

(Pause)

ANNABELLA: *(Meekly)* I was just....

CHARLIE: You was just nothin'! Just don't do it again. *(To himself)* Wreck my fuckin' edge. That's what that stuff could do. My fuckin' edge.

ANNABELLA: Sorry...

CHARLIE: Forget it! Jesus, get me a drink.

ANNABELLA: Sure, Charlie. There's some wine here...

CHARLIE: Yeh. Yeh. Pour it. That'll do.... Now leave me alone. I want some goddamn quiet. O K?

(Pause. ANNABELLA pours a glass of wine from the bottle the WAITER brought. She hands CHARLIE the glass. He sits perfectly, still holding the glass out in front of him. He looks like he is meditating.)

(After a moment, SMITTY enters. He is upset. Angry. Frightened. Pissed off)

ANNABELLA: *(In a whisper)* Smitty, where you been?

SMITTY: *(Loud voice)* I caught up with him, Charlie.

ANNABELLA: Sh-sh! Charlie don't want to be bugged.

SMITTY: Oh, that's too bad. Yeh. But I could care less. 'Cause, man, he's gonna be bugged blue 'til I get some kind of explanation!

(Short pause. CHARLIE hasn't moved.)

SMITTY: See, Charlie, I caught up to him. 'Cause he'd fallen flat on his face. On the sidewalk in front of Woolworth's. The cement. Was crawling on his hands and knees. 'Til he fell again. Then just flopping around on his belly. Oh, a great sight. Yeh. When I got close he was screaming, "Stop him! Stop him!" Great. Awful. Screaming. See, guy, it turned my stomach to watch.

ANNABELLA: Who?

SMITTY: Sleeves!

ANNABELLA: The publisher?

SMITTY: I didn't want to get too close. So I stood in the crowd. We're all silent. Looking. Looking at Sleeves. Unbelievable. Chilling. In seventh grade there was this girl. An epileptic. She sat next to me in general science. Okay. Biggest breasts in class. I couldn't look at 'em. She had three fits by my side. Peanuts compared to Sleeves. Peanuts! See! He dragged his face across the cement. Ripped the skin. Blood. Yeh. Blood. Lots. Pain. Like he was fighting somethin' off. Beat it back. "Stop him!" Who? You want to guess? Huh? I could see his eyes darting. Crazy. Crazy. It was like...I don't know what. He ripped himself up good and two cops took him away.

ANNABELLA: O D'd?

SMITTY: On what? I've been with him.... No. No. Annabella. I don't think so. See, I'm chasing another connection. You still with me, Charlie? Hang in there. Hang in, guy. See, I got a suspicion now that there's more to this conjuring act than I'd suspected. Am I getting warm, Charlie? Hit a nerve?

ANNABELLA: What are you talking about?

SMITTY: Conjuring ain't just some jerk-off fad you're going through, like I thought. Huh, guy? There's too many volts for that. There's a danger sign on the kit. Right? You're playing ball on the warning track, aren't ya?.... Listen, brother, you should know I ain't about to run and jump ship on ya. I've got a stake in this. I'm in this. But I think I should be told if we're moving into a strong current. *I got a right to know what's coming down!!!*

(CHARLIE *has remained still. It now becomes clear that he has been sniffing the wine.*)

CHARLIE: *(Quietly)* Great Western Chablis. *(He doesn't pronounce the 's'.)*

SMITTY: *What?!!* Didn't you hear me?

CHARLIE: *(Still quietly)* Annabella. This wine. Read me its label.

ANNABELLA: *Great Western Chablis.*

SMITTY: Have you heard a fucking word that I've been saying? About Sleeves?

CHARLIE: Annabella. Give me something else to smell. Quick.

ANNABELLA: ...but...

CHARLIE: *(Shouting)* For Christ's sake, hurry!!

SMITTY: Charlie, you tryin' to break my tackle, guy? Is that it? Is that what you're tryin'? To wiggle your butt out of this? Well, if you are. Let me tell you. *It ain't gonna work!!!*

(ANNABELLA *takes the cloth off the tray of smells. She picks out a potato and places it in front of* CHARLIE.)

CHARLIE: *(Matter-of-factly)* A potato. An Idaho potato.

(Brief pause)

ANNABELLA: Yeh. Hey, that's right.

SMITTY: What? He smelled that?

ANNABELLA: *(Ignoring* SMITTY*)* I don't know if it's from Idaho.

CHARLIE: It is. Something else!!

SMITTY: He smelled that?!!!

*(*ANNABELLA *puts a can of soup in front of him.)*

CHARLIE: A can. Soup. Campbell's Cream of Mushroom. Ten and three-quarter ounces. Packaged in New Jersey.

SMITTY: New Jersey?!

CHARLIE: Camden.

ANNABELLA: It's happening. Damn it, it's happening. He's on his way!

*(*SMITTY *has picked up the soup can and looks at the label.)*

SMITTY: On his way where? *Where!!!?*

CHARLIE: *(He smells out everything in front of him—the ashtray, the silverware, then what is on the tray.)* A cigarette butt. Marlboro 100's.... Spoon. Stainless steel. Tablespoon. Made in Japan...Morton's salt...Arm and Hammer Baking Soda...El Rio Taco Shells...Plantation Blackstrap Molasses... Quaker Oats...Log Cabin Maple Syrup...Gulden's spicy brown mustard...

SMITTY: Let me give him something. *(He pulls out a pen.)* Here. Try smelling out this.

ANNABELLA: Put it closer!

CHARLIE: A ballpoint.

SMITTY: *(He starts to take the pen back.)* Yeh. That's right.

CHARLIE: Shaeffer. Black ink.

SMITTY: Okay. Okay.

CHARLIE: Refillable. A dollar ninety-five retail.

SMITTY: That's enough.

CHARLIE: Medium grip.

SMITTY: *(He pulls the pen back.)* I said, *that's enough!* Christ. How did he do that? First Sleeves, then this. Annabella, *how the fuck could he smell that!!!?*

CHARLIE: *(Very still)* The smells.

ANNABELLA: *(To* SMITTY*)* Shut up.

CHARLIE: All of a sudden. They've separated. Separated into distinct blocks. *(The lights have begun to fade, except for a spot on* CHARLIE.*)* It's incredible. Really. Everything now appears to be moving toward a clarity. Into focus. No blurs. No more cross-currents. No gusts. The wind's died down. Movement is slowing down. Unbelievable. Stagnant. Out there. Posed. Like a Rousseau painting of smells. Of tastes. Of sights. *(He takes off his eye patches. The lights continue to fade.)* No more blurred edges. No. None. Honest. No more dulled senses, overlaps. The glass has been wiped clean. All of a sudden, no more harmonies. See, only the basic melody is playing. For me. *(He smiles.)* For you, Charlie. Just for you. Them big doors are set to swing open. Am I right? You can just feel that, can't you? There'll be an open road. There'll be an easy access, a clear field to the main event. To your score, Charlie. Yeh. It's happened. See, it has happened! It's in you!! *(He laughs. The lights continue to fade.)* All of a sudden, The Reporter's High Art is in *you!!* And it'll be working *for* you, Charlie! Tonight! I don't believe it. Say it! It'll be tonight! Say it! Tonight. *Say it! (Blackout except for a spot on* CHARLIE. *He yells:)* Tonight I will conjure!!!!!!!!! *(Suddenly, lights up. As before,* CHARLIE *sits back in his chair, confused, upset; he covers his head. Pause)*

ANNABELLA: Charlie? Charlie, somethin' wrong?

CHARLIE: *(Without looking up)* I don't know.

ANNABELLA: I thought you'd be burstin' now, right? All keyed up, you know? I mean, it's happening, Charlie. Isn't it? It's happening, right?

CHARLIE: *(Turns away)* Give me some space, I don't feel too hot all of a sudden.

ANNABELLA: *(After a short pause, she steps back and glances at* SMITTY.*)* Maybe you're just too excited now, guy. Maybe you're just too hepped up. Maybe that's it.

CHARLIE: *(He suddenly erupts.)* That's not it!!!!!!!!

(He swings his hand across the table and knocks everything to the floor. SMITTY *steps back. Short pause)*

CHARLIE: *(Quietly. mostly to himself)* You know, I don't know why I did that.

(The MAN, *as the lights were fading, stood up and put on his coat and hat. He now approaches* CHARLIE.*)*

MAN: Charlie? *(He shuffles the file cards.)*

ANNABELLA: *(To* SMITTY*)* Who the hell's that?

*(*SMITTY *shakes his head.)*

MAN: I overheard what you're up to, Charlie.

CHARLIE: So what?

ANNABELLA: Look, he don't wanta be pestered, okay?

MAN: *(Ignoring her)* And I just wanted to wish you well tonight.

*(*CHARLIE *looks up at him.)*

ANNABELLA: That's nice. That's real nice. I'm sure Charlie appreciates that.

(She tries to move him along.)

MAN: That is, of course, if you are still planning to work tonight. I didn't misunderstand you, did I, Charlie?

CHARLIE: What the hell is that supposed to mean?! Jesus, what biz is it of yours, anyway?

ANNABELLA: Come on, mister. I don't wanta have to call the waiter.

MAN: It's just that, at the moment, correct me if I am wrong, Charlie, but at this precise moment, you don't seem terrible excited about your 'project'.

*(*CHARLIE *waves* ANNABELLA *away.)*

MAN: You aren't having second thoughts, are you, Charlie?

CHARLIE: Look, mister. I'm fuckin thrilled, right? I can't wait, okay? Inside, I'm bouncin', see! Just 'cause I don't wear it on my god damn sleeve!!

MAN: Excellent. Excellent. That's all I wanted to know. Then, I wish you well, Charlie. I'll be pulling for you.

*(*MAN *exits. Pause)*

CHARLIE: *(To* ANNABELLA *and* SMITTY; *yells) I'm fucking thrilled!!!!!*

(Blackout)

END OF ACT ONE

ACT TWO

(Stage dark. Pause)

(A small fire is started center stage. Lights up on a study. CHARLIE's apartment. Center: a large desk facing downstage. A small wastebasket is on the desk. The fire is in this wastebasket. A number of chairs, a lamp or two, piles of old newspapers and newsmagazines, etc.—around. CHARLIE, without eye patches, sits behind his desk, asleep. He wears a bright red track suit. SMITTY and ANNABELLA stand feeding the fire with pieces of paper—CHARLIE's manuscript; ANNABELLA has a metal poker. She shreds the paper while SMITTY is bunching up a number of pieces at once and tossing them into the flames. Both speak softly so as not to wake up CHARLIE. Pause)

SMITTY: This is a bum idea, Annabella. A zero, see. But what I think don't seem to matter much around here anymore.

ANNABELLA: Don't crumple them up like that. They won't burn good that way.

SMITTY: When did you become an expert? *(Pause. He keeps on bunching up the paper.)* We're taking down our backstop. That's what we're doing now, ya know. That's just what Charlie's having us do. It's crazy. It don't make sense. We'll have nothin' to fall back on.

ANNABELLA: Who's falling back, guy?

SMITTY: *(Trying to ignore her)* What I don't see is why we have to give up one direction just 'cause Charlie's into another. Ain't he ever heard about insurance? Jesus, we haven't even run all the business heats yet. I still got the feeling there could have been a nice score in this manuscript. We seemed close with Sleeves, didn't we?

ANNABELLA: But there's a bigger score coming, Smitty. Ya got to remember that. And ya got to figure on giving up something to make that kind of run.

SMITTY: Yeh. Sure. Sure. So we get rid of past angles like this book—as a necessary step, to lighten the load. So Charlie says. Yeh. But does Charlie say anything about the danger signs posted along that route? You don't know nothin' about that fact, Annabella, but I do!

ANNABELLA: All the signs Charlie sees say "Go"!

SMITTY: Are you really sure of that?

ANNABELLA: What's that supposed to mean?

SMITTY: It's just that, for a guy who says he's set up so great. You know. Charlie's always said he had to be one hundred percent to even approach this act. Well, he ain't been actin' one hundred percent has he?

ANNABELLA: He's been lookin' fine to me.

SMITTY: You may call the way he's been actin' tonight "fine", but I don't.

ANNABELLA: Smitty, that's all just part of the game plan. Somethin' Charlie's gotta move through.

SMITTY: Maybe. Yeh. Sure. Maybe that's all that it is. I can figure that. But all I'm saying is that if Charlie's gotta go, then okay, go. Go. But go slow. I ain't discounting the score here. I ain't saying that. How could I? I saw what he did with those smells back at the club. I don't understand it. But I saw. But all I'm really saying is that I ain't sure a score is guaranteed right now neither. That this is the best time. So why don't he take it easy. Wait a week or so. Let whatever has happened be given time to settle in. Then we wouldn't have to take down this backstop 'til we're double sure he's ready. That's all. Right now, I just think Charlie's moving too fast.

ANNABELLA: Too fast for you, maybe.

SMITTY: That's just what I'm saying. Too fast for me. For my taste. My nerves.

ANNABELLA: But you don't really think Charlie's gonna pull up one beat 'cause of what you think?

(CHARLIE *groans.*)

ANNABELLA: He's coming around.

CHARLIE: (*Waking up; hardly understandable*) Involvement. Involvement. Tonight...

ANNABELLA: (*She shoves the remainder of the manuscript into the fire*) Come on. He said he wanted some time to himself when he came to. (*She starts to exit.*) Come on.

SMITTY: Wait a minute. I wanta talk with him.

CHARLIE: (*Yelling*) *Because tonight! Tonight...!* (*Awake.* CHARLIE *is shaken. Short pause. He sees* SMITTY *and* ANNABELLA.) I thought I said I wanted to be alone. God damn it, what do I have to do? Spell everything out? Leave me alone! (*He screams at them.*) *Leave me alone!!* (*He covers his head with his hands.*)

ANNABELLA: (*To* SMITTY) Come on.

(SMITTY *hesitates.*)

SMITTY: (*To* ANNABELLA) You see what I mean?

(ANNABELLA *and* SMITTY *exit.*)

CHARLIE: Tonight. Tonight what? I don't know. That's right, I don't know. Crazy. Yeh. Crazy dream, all right. *(He relaxes a bit and removes his hands from his face.)* Charlie. Get this. Get a hold of yourself and get this, guy. Do you know who you were in your dream? Huh, Charlie? What do you make of this? You...was...the fucking *New York Times*. Yeh, Charlie, the *Times*. The whole god damn thing!... Yeh. Me. What do you think, Charlie? I don't know. Could just show how close you are. How ready. Yeh. The *Times*. Show how confident I am. How set. Maybe. Maybe.... But then why am I shaking? *(Short pause)* Let's see. I was sitting. I was sitting here checking out my rhythm and reflexes. Concentrating on reflexes. 'Cause they're gonna be a big tool in a conjuring act. Or so I suspect. Reactions gonna have to be fast. Right. Okay, I was doing a reflex power bit. To get myself prepped. For tonight.... Then what? Then I shot asleep. And started running. In an alley. Broken glass. Winos passed out. Women beating rugs. I'm sprinting. But it's easy. No effort. I come across a crowd of guys. Twenty or thirty. Just hanging around. But all look bushed. Panting. Their tongues out. Baggy pants. Cheap suits. Just standin' about. I recognize three of 'em. *Boston Globe. Chicago Tribune. Philadelphia Inquirer.* They smile at me. But don't say nothin'. I feel sad for a moment, but a bus comes by and takes me away. I walk into a modern office building. No windows. Steel. No ventilation. Everyone is smoking up a storm. The noise gives me an earache. Deafening. I carry an umbrella. Some fellas sip coffee by the water cooler. They shout something. Hands waving. I can't hear. I get closer. They ask if it's raining outside. They introduce themselves as *New York Daily News*, L A *Times*, and *Washington Post*. We shake hands. Their palms hot and damp from the coffee. Their sleeves rolled up. Bags under their eyes. Smoking. Puffs. Clouds. I choke. Cigarette burns down their arms. Scars. I put a handkerchief over my mouth. I catch a taxi to the roof. This is my office. Above the timber line. Fantastic view of the ocean. I notice that it's been quiet when the phone rings. The caller asks for *The New York Times*. I tell him: that's me. I read him the sign on my desk: "I've got the best reflexes in the biz. I'm the quickest to react. Can move better from an event outward than anyone else in the whole journalistic field. Some event happens—zap— my reaction fast as lightning." Goodbye. I hang up. I start to giggle. So I'm the fucking *Times*. I put my feet up on my desk. Smoke a Cuban stogie. So I'm the *Times*. And I ain't even winded. I start a letter. To my readers. For the front page. "Dear Reader. The *Times* Announces! After Months of Self-Examination. After Striking Conclusions...." I start again. "Dear Reader." For the final edition. In *Times* type. "The *Times* Announces A Shift in Policy! A Change of Angle! A New Stance and Handle! Dear Friends! Dear Readers? It Is Now The *Times*' Hope! The *Times*' Dream! The *Times*' Driving Ambition! That No One Is Ever Gonna Say Again!—Never!—That The Fucking *New York Times* Lacks Involvement! Involvement *(Screams, out of control) Nobody!!!! 'Cause Tonight, See, Tonight I'm Gonna Conjure!!!!!! (Taken aback by his outburst,* CHARLIE, *upset, covers his head with his hands.*

Short pause) What the...? Conjure. Yeh. Sure. *(Short pause)* I got this feeling, Charlie, that there is something about this that you ain't quite grasped.

(The MAN *of ACT ONE enters dressed as an* OLD 1930's REPORTER—*baggy pants, white shirt, brimmed hat with a press card stuck in it.* CHARLIE *will not recognize this reporter as the* MAN. CHARLIE *doesn't notice him until he speaks.)*

OLD REPORTER: Hello, Charlie.

CHARLIE: *(Startled)* Who the hell are you?.... What are you, from some weekly?

(OLD REPORTER *doesn't respond.)*

CHARLIE: Listen, I don't know what the fuck you're doing in here. I don't know why they let you in. Annabella probably thought it'd be real nice to get some eye on this act. She's been after that for a long time. But believe me, this ain't the time, fella. Okay? Right now I don't want nobody hangin' around while I'm gettin myself together. You with me? Now beat it out of here.... Did you hear me?!

OLD REPORTER: I hear you're gonna try to conjure, Charlie.

CHARLIE: She tell you that too? Well, yeh, I might. Now scram, will you?

OLD REPORTER: You know you ain't the first to make this kind of run, Charlie.

CHARLIE: I thought I said scram!.... Jesus, are you deaf?

OLD REPORTER: You ain't the first to have the urge, Charlie. The hunger. Push. To wanta erase the foul line. The out of bounds. Move out of the pocket. Throw away the book of rules. No limits. No holds barred. No end. No whistles.

CHARLIE: Who the hell *are* you? Who told you about me?

OLD REPORTER: Back in 1960, a novelist-turned-reporter tried this trick—he ended up stabbing his wife in the middle of a New York street. He got off lucky—just a couple of months in Bellevue. You might not be so lucky, Charlie.

CHARLIE: So you're educated in the past moves of this ballgame. So what?... That don't give you no right to come busting in here.

OLD REPORTER: There's a lot more. In 1970, Ed Sanders over-amping on the Manson murders came real close to lying expired in the trunk of a car— doing permanent meditation next to a tire. But he pulled out in time. Smart fella, he was.

CHARLIE: Don't you think I know that! Christ. But Ed, see, didn't have the reflexes I do. Though sure I gotta admire his guts. What are you after, pal!

OLD REPORTER: There's Talese, who's spent the last six years throwing himself deeper and deeper into a sexual-mores-in-America trip. Last seen, he was commuting between a massage parlor on 39th Street and a nudist camp in New Jersey. His friends say, Charlie, he is stuck for good. He ain't ever gonna come up for air.

CHARLIE: I don't know what your angle is, buster...

OLD REPORTER: In 1971, a former sports writer—like yourself, Charlie— he razzled and dazzled as he mainlined America with a Vegas number. You can't say he wasn't prepared. He's got scars from that venture, Charlie, and he ain't even felt all the effects yet.

CHARLIE: *(Really nervous)* Who says he hasn't? Huh? I know Hunter and if he's still stinging then it's cause he hadn't practiced like I have. But wait just a minute!

OLD REPORTER: And that's just a few of the big guns. There are hundreds of *small* frys like yourself, Charlie, whose fates were never documented.

CHARLIE: *(Upset)* Small frys! Jesus Christ, man! Now that's it! That does it! You've gone too far now!

OLD REPORTER: The question is: Will you, Charlie?

CHARLIE: Huh?

OLD REPORTER: Will you go too far.

CHARLIE: What the fuck are you after, anyway? Did someone set you up for this? Is that it? *(He has stood up, pacing.)* To throw me off the goddamn track? Subvert my confidence? Is that it? Stand still when I'm talking to you!

OLD REPORTER: I'm not the one who is moving, Charlie.

CHARLIE: What? *(He stops pacing for a beat; confused.)*

OLD REPORTER: Maybe you should take a step back and look at yourself, guy.

CHARLIE: Me? I am looking. And I'm looking good!

(OLD REPORTER has taken out of his pocket a stack of red three-by-five file cards with a ribbon around them. He places them on CHARLIE's desk. CHARLIE does not notice this.)

OLD REPORTER: Total involvement: That's no light sport, Charlie. I just thought I should warn you. *(He turns to exit.)*

CHARLIE: You warn me! Get out! Throwing out doubts. Jesus! (CHARLIE *picks up the poker* ANNABELLA *had been using and threatens the* OLD REPORTER.) You want a smack in the face! *Get the hell out?!!*

(OLD REPORTER exits whistling.)

CHARLIE: *(Upset, pacing again; after a pause)* Jesus. What the fuck was he...? Talking like a history book. Last month's scratch sheet. What was he after? Huh? Bringing up Hunter, Norman, Gay, Ed. Okay. Okay. They were good. Right. And they got crunched. Sure. But so what? *So what!* What's that got to do with me? Here. They weren't set. They weren't practiced. They all just fell into their involvement acts. Not me. I'm set, right? I've studied, right? I've trained, right? *Well, haven't I?...* He warn me. I'll show him. *I'll fuckin' show him!!* Annabella! Smitty!

(ANNABELLA *enters.)*

CHARLIE: Let's get this show on the road! Let's fuckin' roll!

ANNABELLA: Sure, guy. What can I do?

CHARLIE: Where's Smitty?

SMITTY: *(Entering)* Right here, Charlie.

CHARLIE: Great. Now let's get all this crap pushed back. I'm gonna need room for this. Lots of fuckin' space. And light. I want every goddamn light I own in here. Okay? So let's move it!

(CHARLIE *paces, pleased.* ANNABELLA *begins to push back the chairs, piles of papers, etc.* SMITTY, *still worried, doesn't move and stares at* CHARLIE.)

ANNABELLA: Smitty!

(SMITTY *hesitates, then slowly goes to help* ANNABELLA—*though he continues to watch* CHARLIE.)

CHARLIE: *(Smiling; to himself)* That old guy did you a big favor, Charlie. Course he didn't mean to. That's for sure. But he did just the same. He fuckin' got your goat, guy. And that's all that was needed. *(Laughs)* All Charlie needed. Shit. One minute you're down, watching some joker try to tie your shoelaces together. Then the next. The next. I'm back on top. I'm set up good. He had no idea. I'll show him. I'll show him something all right.

(ANNABELLA *and* SMITTY *are on opposite sides of a big chair and try to lift it off.)*

ANNABELLA: Pick it up, Smitty.

SMITTY: Shut up.

CHARLIE: *(To* ANNABELLA *and* SMITTY*)* By the way, why *did* you let that crazy old guy in here? I did tell you both I wanted to be left alone.

ANNABELLA: *(Looking around)* What old guy?

CHARLIE: The old guy who just ran out of here. I'm surprised he didn't run ya both down. He did a big peel out bit when I went after him with this. *(He holds up the poker.)*

ANNABELLA: I didn't see nobody. Smitty?

SMITTY: Not a soul, Charlie.

CHARLIE: Are you two joking or somethin'? If you are, that ain't very funny.

ANNABELLA: I'll go get the lights. *(She starts to exit.)*

CHARLIE: Wait a minute. He was just right here. Standing there. I talked with him. *(He is getting nervous.)* But neither of you saw him.

ANNABELLA: Maybe he's still in the room.

CHARLIE: I said I chased him out!

*(*CHARLIE *smashes the poker against the desk. Short pause.* SMITTY *and* ANNABELLA *look at each other, concerned for* CHARLIE. CHARLIE *starts to pace again.)*

SMITTY: Look, Charlie. You're seemin' a touch shakey, guy. Maybe you ought to calm down a beat before you actually begin the act.

CHARLIE: *Stand still!!*

*(*ANNABELLA *and* SMITTY *look at each other, confused.)*

ANNABELLA: You know, Charlie, maybe Smitty is right. What about a rubdown, guy? How does that sound? Could cool the pressure.

CHARLIE: *Stop that mumbling!*

SMITTY: A slight postponement, guy. That's all I've been calling for all along.

(Short pause. CHARLIE *stops pacing. He stares at* ANNABELLA *and* SMITTY.*)*

CHARLIE: Oh. Now I get it. Yeh, now I really get it. A slight postponement, huh? Boy, am I slow. Shit! You two must really take me for a dodo! So that is your move, is it. Jesus, I should have guessed.

ANNABELLA: What is, Charlie?

CHARLIE: *(Pacing again)* That is your angle. Of course. Of course. It took me a while. It really did. Well, I may be slow, but I ain't thick. Anything to puncture my urge, right? You'd do anything, right?

ANNABELLA: What are you talking about?

CHARLIE: You let that buster in here. To wreck my confidence. My edge. To turn me loose on myself. Yeh. You might have even planned the whole thing. Though I doubt that. You two ain't bright enough for that. No. And then when that act didn't work. When that move fell flat on its face, now you're all set to play deaf and dumb. Try to get me to think I am losing my mind. That I'm seeing things. Right? Well, I haven't fallen for it, see! It has not worked, see! *(Laughs)*

ANNABELLA: We're behind you, guy.

SMITTY: I think that's what he's afraid of.

CHARLIE: Right when I'm on the verge. Razor sharp. Well, it's my own fault. I should have guessed Charlie'd get blocked from the inside. Least I stopped this check in time. Yeh. Nice Charlie. Nice action. Good reflex there. Good work. There is no way I'm gonna postpone shit now. No way. *No way! You hear me!*

ANNABELLA: Sure, guy.

CHARLIE: I've been rocking on my heels gettin' set to run. I'm tired of interruptions and cheap shots. I'm knee deep in motion and that's that.

ANNABELLA: Sure. You're calling the signals, guy.

CHARLIE: What?

ANNABELLA: I said, you're calling the signals, Charlie.

CHARLIE: You can bet your ass I am. *And* I'm playing all the parts too. This ain't no team game. See. It's a one-man-show routine. There's room at the top for one and one only. I should have figured that out a long time ago. I don't need you! Is that straight?

ANNABELLA: Yeh, Charlie.

CHARLIE: Good. Now get the hell out!

ANNABELLA: *(Hurt)* What?

CHARLIE: I can move cleaner without worrying you two are gonna do a backstabbing duet. Did you hear me?

SMITTY: *(Wants to talk)* Charlie...

CHARLIE: That goes for you too. *I said get out!*

(ANNABELLA *and* SMITTY *exit.* CHARLIE, *upset, pacing)*

CHARLIE: *(To himself)* Boy, do they got their nerve. What fucking nerve. Christ. Yeh. Who'd have believed this? Who'd have believed I'd have to protect my rear? I expect a strong backup and I get drowned out. Get booed by my own goddamn bench! *(He stops pacing; calm tone of voice.)* That's enough crabbin', Charlie. I think that's just plenty. Now take it easy. So this ain't how you pictured your opening, right? So what? You expected butterflies and you got bats, so what? *(He quickly turns toward where* ANNABELLA *and* SMITTY *exited and shouts.)* I thought I told you two to get out! *(No one is there; calm tone continuing)* You got a hide, don't you? Your balance ain't so delicate as all that, is it? They didn't make no real crack, did they? *(He erupts, upset.)* Yes, they did. God damnit! Look at me. *Look at me!* *(Short pause; calm)* Now listen, Charlie. You had a plan for this, didn't you? So where is it? Let's find it. You had a rhythm building, right? Believe me, you did, guy. You still got the urge. I know you do. You're still in the running, right? You ain't been scratched yet, have you? *(Upset)* Maybe I have. I ain't exactly coasting along, am I?... Don't talk like that.... See for yourself. Look at me.... I am looking, and you're looking good.... Look at me!.... Shut up!.... Stand still *and look!...* Shut up! *I said shut up!!* (*Long pause; he stands still, smiling*) Now ain't that somethin'? I'm arguing. No one here. Me. I'm arguing with me. Me is arguing with me. (*He laughs.*) That's great. That's just swell. That says a lot, don't it. Says the whole thing right there. Christ. The whole thing in a goddamn nutshell. (*Laughs; this laugh turns into a scream:*) *What am I doing!!!* What do I do now? (*He leans over his desk. Covers his head*)

(MAN *enters, still dressed as an* OLD REPORTER. CHARLIE *does not see him and in no way acknowledges or responds to him.*)

OLD REPORTER: Don't read those cards, Charlie.

(CHARLIE *notices the red file cards for the first time.*)

OLD REPORTER: Don't touch them. There is still time, guy. Time to reflect. Time to pull up. To pull on the cord. Time to take a step back and regain that perspective, Charlie. That overview. From the outside. From where you belong. Where you fit in. Your natural element.

(CHARLIE *picks up the cards, unties the ribbon.*)

OLD REPORTER: There is still time to check out the book of rules. Time to chalk back in the lines you've rubbed out. Get the fences back up. Time still to call time for order. To clear the field. Clear you mind. Time to keep your distance. Your natural distance.

(CHARLIE *begins to look through the cards.*)

OLD REPORTER: Don't look at those cards! Look at yourself, Charlie. Go ahead and look. Where is that detached look? The look of the onlooker? Of the low-lying recorder? The natural reporter.

CHARLIE: Whose handwriting is this?

OLD REPORTER: Look at yourself. You're a natural reporter, do you really want to be a player, Charlie?

(OLD REPORTER *laughs and exits.*)

CHARLIE: These are weird. (*Reads*) "Charlie, you've done your homework as best as it could be done. You get straight A's. You make the honor roll. You've worked your tail off getting set for this number. As reporters go, you're the tops. You're great, man." Who wrote these? "Ain't nobody can cover an event like you can. You got all the angles. You got every base covered. You're in the majors. You're at your best form. You're in the position everyone wants to be in. You're great. Yeh, you're great." Who the hell wrote these? (*He begins to get into these cards, starts by enjoying them, and slowly goes almost into a trance because of them.*) "You're the boss-man and everyone loves you. They need you. They dream they are you and have your good moves. They listen to what you say. They copy your angles. They take your advice. They feel lucky to have known you or been in the same room as you. You get results. You're great. You're great." Yeh. "You are the leader-man. Way ahead of the field. Avant garde. The other's way in. You stand between them and what's big. You're the connection. You determine what's big by where you play. You're great." Yeh. "You could have taken an easier road. It was open to you. But you struck out on your own. Held your own. Cleared your own field. Found your own stance and grip. You're great." Yeh. "If you can't get involved nobody else can, either. You're great." Yeh. "You're the favorite. The smart money's on you. You're in a class by yourself. You're great." Yeh. "You are the fair-haired boy and you are the old master. You are great, man. You are great! You're great!" Yeh. *(He sets the cards down. He is a bit drowsy.)* There. That was nice. Real nice. All I needed was a little goddamn appreciation. Every once in a while. Who wouldn't, huh? A nice pat on the back.... Who wrote...? *(He almost falls asleep. He is now possessed by another voice:)* I am ready to see what only I can see. What only a trained eye can perceive. I have that eye. I am ready to hear before there is anything even to be heard. To hear that something is about to be heard. I have such an ear. I am ready. *(In his own voice; very sleepy)* Wait a...Charlie? I wouldn't go quite that far. I mean...what do I mean? I mean, there's no rush, right? What's the hurry? I mean, aren't I still sort of stinging from them geeks? *(Other voice)* I am ready to smell before there is anything out there to smell. I am ready to find expression for all smells in my smelling. To find expression for all sights in my ability to see them. I am ready. *(In his own voice, trying to stay awake)* Look. We'll try this act. Sure we will. But some other time, okay? In a little while. Right now, I just.... I just.... I wanta catch a little shut-eye.... *(Other voice)* I have reported on a thousand events. But never before from this angle. Never before from the inside position. The inside looking out. Give me your scoops. Your confessions. Your history and your passions. And I will express them for you. *(In his own voice)* I thought I said.... Slow down.... come on and slow down.... I just wanta.... I wanta sleep... *(He "falls asleep", his head on the desk. Other voice)* All that was needed was a clean route of escape. And now there is one. All that was needed was a trained medium and I am that. I am that medium. *(He calmly picks up the poker, that is, it is the personality behind the other voice that picks up the poker. Then, suddenly and violently, he smashes it against the desk, against the same spot where* CHARLIE *had just layed his head. "Own voice" screams out in pain, holds his head. Other voice)* As I said, now I am ready. *(Giggles, short pause)* I am ready to conjure. *(He calmly looks around, takes in the territory, then yells)* I will conjure!!! *(There is a flash powder explosion—bang/smoke. Also, on tape, the sound of a bomb, or a sonic boom. At the moment of the explosion he starts to cough and choke violently. He collapses across his desk. When he later picks up his head, blood is seen running out of his mouth. Pause)*

(The MAN *enters, taking off his* OLD REPORTER *costume; he now wears a baseball-type cap, blazer, white shirt, etc. He walks slowly to* CHARLIE. *As in the tradition of*

*other great coaches, Lombardi, Hayes, Bryant, he will now be simply called—*COACH.*)*

COACH: On a scale of one to ten, Charlie. One to ten. I'd have to tag that opening a three, son. Which ain't quite as bad as it sounds. I mean, it ain't exactly all-pro or somethin'. Ain't all what I expected when you caught my eye back at the club. But least you're off the block and that's what really counts now, don't it? At this time, I mean. Them big numbers, they're just gonna have to be flashed later. But for now, Charlie, it's a start. It's a start. And that's what matters, right, son?

CHARLIE: *(Still choking; picks up his head)* What are you doing here? *(Notices the blood on his face)*

COACH: Just call me Coach, sonny. Coach.

CHARLIE: I'm bleeding.

*(*COACH *is now behind* CHARLIE. *He grabs* CHARLIE's *hair and pulls back his head.)*

COACH: Let me see that. Heck, boy. Heck. Nothin' to piss about there. *(He lets go.)* No good reason to pull yourself there. Oughta make ya just that much more determined. Get you to grit the hell down and bite the bullet. Just put some spit on it and you'll think you're sweating. Wear it, son, don't go fawnin' over it! Don't be no candy-ass, Charlie. What'll people think?

CHARLIE: I'm bleeding!

COACH: And you're whining. That's what you're doing, kid. And, boy, do we hate whiners. Hate their guts, Charlie. 'Cause they got no balls, boy. No pride. Good for shit down the stretch. Under fire. Worthless human beings who don't pull their own weight, so the rest of us suckers gotta carry 'em along. You follow me, Charlie? People don't like to look at whiners, pal. They make 'em sick. Now tell me, boy, you ain't one of them, are you? *(He picks up* CHARLIE's *head again by the hair.)*

CHARLIE *(Shaking his head)* No, I ain't....

COACH: *(He lets go of* CHARLIE's *head.)* Well, that's a good thing. That's a real relief all right. Afraid for a minute I'd read you all wrong. Afraid you were gonna let all them people down, boy. But nah, Charlie, he's no crybaby, he's no spineless jerk. He's got the prick to match that strut. He's got a God-given talent *and he's gonna use it!* Come on, son—*it's your god damn duty to use it!* Now get tough! Get tough!... So tell me, boy, what's your next move?

CHARLIE: In a minute. Just give me a minute. Let me rest...

COACH: You are trying my patience, pal! Listen, Charlie, if you wanta play in this game you gotta be a lot tougher than you're actin'. You wanta play, you gotta produce. You can't go runnin' off to the showers every other minute. Can't go hide under the fuckin' bench. This is the big leagues,

Charlie! The god damn big top! There are people out there waiting for you! What are they going to think, son? What are they thinkin' right this second? Where's your self-respect, boy? *Show us your self-respect and let's go!*

CHARLIE: What people?

COACH: Are you kiddin', Charlie? *What* people? That's a pretty dumb-ass joke if you are. There are millions waiting, Charlie. Millions!

CHARLIE: Where?

COACH: Out there! Out there! *Listen*!!

(On tape, sound of a large stadium crowd chanting, "Go-Go-Go". After a few seconds, tape off.)

CHARLIE: *(Stunned; confused)* How did you do that?

COACH: I said *listen!!*

(On tape, sound of a large stadium crowd chanting, "CHARLIE-CHARLIE-CHARLIE". Tape off. CHARLIE is in shock.)

COACH: See what I mean, pal? They're out there. Waiting for you. You don't want to let them down now. They want to hear from you, pal. See you. Watch you. Smell you. Cheer you on! You're somethin' to them. They're out there right now looking for *you!* They're eager. Hungry. Anxious. Little girls on daddies' shoulders. Old men with canes and straw hats. Kids sittin' on flag poles. Pennants waving. Horns honking. Peanut vendors yelling. Policemen directing traffic. Spotlights, Charlie! Searchlights! They are all looking for you! More and more are joining the crowd every second. Joining the crushing mass every split second! Don't let them down, Charlie! You are their connection! You've got their attention! They are waiting! You are the attraction! The main attraction! Don't let us down, Charlie! *Don't let us down!*

(CHARLIE begins to breathe heavily.)

COACH: You're no quitter, pal. I can tell that just by lookin' at you. Knew it the first time I laid eyes on you. You got spunk, kid. You got nerve. Daring. Now just get out there and get tough! *Get tough!*

(CHARLIE begins to breathe more heavily.)

COACH: You're no second-stringer, pal. You don't have to dirty your jersey in the locker room. You've got class, son. You've got talent. Now just get tough! Yes! *I said, get tough!*

(CHARLIE starts to stand up.)

COACH: That-a-way pal! That's the spirit! Show your self-respect! Be a man, boy! Be a man. *Be a man!*

CHARLIE: *(In shock, other voice)* I confess. I never wanted to be nothin' except a reporter. I confess....

COACH: Good. Good. A personal angle. That's putting yourself on the line, son. That should get you running. They'll like that. Yeh, they'll like that. Now just keep it going, boy. *Keep it going...!*

CHARLIE: As a kid I'd stand alone every year at my birthday party, watching the local kids do their fun and games. I confess I could only participate from a distance. Only deal at arm's length. My thoughts and feelings mesh perfectly with the Reporter's rhythm. I confess it's true. And it's always been true for me! And I confess I have fed off other folks' actions. Their wrongs, scandals, joys, hardships, triumphs, new buildings, and last-place finishes. And I confess I have survived on other folks' handiwork. Their murals, maps, muggings, prints and perfect swings, interior designs and leaps of faith. I confess I have lived from their hands to my mouth. But isn't reporting an action of equal or greater weight? *I think it must be!* I confess! I turned pro at age fifteen, which is young in this league. My first job was as a sportswriter down in Dixie. Jesus, the names I could throw out. The people I've stood next to! I've got Gale Yarborough's autograph right here! *(He points to his head.)* Anyone want to see? I confess! It's all I ever wanted to be! *I confess!*

COACH: *(Obviously pleased)* Okay. Okay. Heck. That's more like it. That's applying yourself. That's more like what we're expecting to see. Now don't that feel better, boy? Sure it does, heck. Now we're cooking. Now we're cooking.

CHARLIE: *(Stunned, in his own voice)* Look, mister...

COACH: Coach.

CHARLIE: Yeh. Look, Coach, I don't have the faintest idea what is coming down now. Couldn't we, I mean...let's talk about this, okay?

(COACH picks up a towel.)

COACH: Here, dry yourself off.

(He throws the towel to CHARLIE. CHARLIE ignores it. He begins to breathe heavily.)

CHARLIE: *(Other voice)* The Reporter has more muscle than Paul Hornung or Bubba Smith. The Reporter has more grace than a Peggy Fleming. The Reporter has more art than a Pablo Picasso or Casals. The Reporter has more spunk than a featherweight on the way up.

COACH: *(Chuckling)* Run with it, boy. Run with it.

CHARLIE: The Reporter has more range than a Beverly Sills ever had. More gusto than an H H H ever had. More potential than a Tom Tresh ever had. More rhythm than Otis ever had, more draw than Jagger ever had, more power than Billy Graham ever had! The Reporter has more class than any high-strutting dude in Harlem *or* Scarsdale. And he lives right around the corner. *I am him! I confess!*

(Another flash, powder explosion. Also, on tape, the sounds of a stadium crowd cheering. This stays on for a few moments. At the sound of the explosion, CHARLIE screams in pain at the top of his lungs, though he does not collapse. The COACH laughs. ANNABELLA and SMITTY run in. They can never see COACH.)

ANNABELLA: Charlie. You okay? We heard you scream. What's the matter, guy?

(CHARLIE is in shock.)

SMITTY: Oh, shit. He's cracked up good. Look at him.

ANNABELLA: Charlie? Charlie? He doesn't even hear me. Snap out of it, guy. Snap out. Maybe he's asleep, Smitty.

SMITTY: Are you nuts, too? Look at him! You don't sleep standing up with your eyes open! He's gone under. Simple as that. Way under in deep water. And don't say I didn't warn you something like this would happen. Jesus.

ANNABELLA: Hey, guy. Try to sit down. Bend your legs. Come on. You hear me, sit down! Charlie!

SMITTY: I saw it coming. I could feel the risk in this angle from the start. He was moving too fast. But, no, you wouldn't listen to me, would you? Now look what's happened!

ANNABELLA: *Shut up!...* Maybe if we got him a glass of water or a blanket or something.

SMITTY: Yeh. Right. That'd be a real big help. *We don't even know what he's done!* I should have played my instincts from the top and sabotaged this run long ago.

ANNABELLA: *Shut up!...* He'll come out of it. Any second and he'll come out of it.

COACH: Come on, Charlie. I think that's enough rest, don't you, son? We don't wanta get the cramps, boy. We can't afford to let up now. We gotta keep that pressure on. Keep that momentum on our side!

CHARLIE: *(Scared, in his own voice—ANNABELLA and SMITTY cannot hear him.)* Listen, I don't know who the hell you are....

COACH: Coach. Just call me Coach.

CHARLIE: Yeh. I got that. But what the fuck is happening to me!

COACH: You wanted to conjure, Charlie. What's the matter, guy? Didn't you hear that crowd? They love you. They're mad about you. You're a big fucking hit, guy!

CHARLIE: I want to stop this!

COACH: You had your chances for that, Charlie.... Now come on, son! Keep pressing! *Keep pressing!*

CHARLIE: What's to stop me from walking out of here?

(COACH *laughs.*)

ANNABELLA: I think he's moving his lips!

SMITTY: I don't hear nothin'.

ANNABELLA: Sh-sh!

CHARLIE: *(In a panic) Stop this!!!!*

COACH: *(Screams) Play ball!!!!!*

CHARLIE: *(Other voice—*ANNABELLA *and* SMITTY *hear this.)* Shapes arise.

ANNABELLA: There.

SMITTY: Yeh. What's he saying?

ANNABELLA: I don't know. Be quiet!

CHARLIE: *(Other voice)* Shapes arise. Shapes of old events and new events and events on the way. Shapes of printing presses, satellites, control rooms, scribes, news rooms, press conferences. Shapes of headlines and obituaries and comics and box scores. Shapes of humor and of death. Shapes of the crowd in Times Square waiting for the news. Shapes of faces, hands, words, letters, ink. Shapes in motion and at rest.

(COACH *chuckles.*)

SMITTY: I don't get it.

CHARLIE: *(Continuing)* Shapes arise. Shapes of logs and liquids, of pulp and of steam. Shapes of black rollers getting blacker by the rhythmic beat. Shapes of empires being plotted in pins on a map. Shapes of foldings and of mergers. Shapes of copy boys, editors, cub reporters, owners, readers, and distributors. Shapes of classifieds. Shapes of wants. Desires. Openings. Dreams. Shapes of newspapers being bundled on an empty train in the middle of the night.
Shapes arise! The same shapes again and again. The only shapes of the main event. *The one event!* ...But it has many heads.

(COACH *claps lightly, smiles.*)

(Short pause)

(ANNABELLA *and* SMITTY *look at each other, speechless.*)

ANNABELLA: Maybe he's...

SMITTY: Go ahead. I'm listening. I can't wait to hear what kind of explanation you're gonna pull out for this. I'm waiting. *What the hell is he talking about?!!!!!*

ANNABELLA: *(Almost in tears)* I don't know.

COACH: As they say—you ain't gonna swim til you're thrown in. Into the fucking deep end! *So let's keep pushing!!!*

CHARLIE: *(Breathing heavily: other voice)* I watch the Super Bowl and the crowd they cheer me. Break my neck getting to a fire and the fire it waits for me. I interview the candidate and the candidate, he questions me. As will his opponent. Why? *(This other voice is becoming more and more animated, more of another personality)* I discover the scandal and the world discovers me. I stand behind the camera but *my* face is on the film. Why should that be? I listen to the policy statement and it comes out in my name, my style, my voice. My personal point of view. Why?

SMITTY: *(To* ANNABELLA*)* You still thinking, he's gonna pop out any second?

ANNABELLA: *I said, I don't know!!!!!!*

SMITTY: Look, I'm gonna shut him up before he dives any deeper!

ANNABELLA: No! *Don't touch him!!*

*(*SMITTY *stops.)*

ANNABELLA: Maybe you'd hurt him, ya know? Stopping him like that. All of a sudden.

SMITTY: *(Moving away)* If you ask me, he looks real hurt already.

COACH: I think you're getting the knack of it, Charlie. Nice. Just real nice, boy. But don't stop there. *Don't stop there!!!*

CHARLIE: *(Other voice)* Why? Because events exist for me to witness. For me. They have no meaning by themselves. Armstrong walked on the moon for me. Sadat flies to Israel for me. Ford builds its Mustang and Pinto for me. The United States Government will rise and fall for me as will every government past, present, or future. "Blond on Blond" was written and sung for me. Ali whipped Foreman for me. Burton will get back with Liz for me. The headwaiter at Sans Souci holds a table for me. The West was won for me. The campuses they erupted for me. Nothing would be out there if not for me! *I confess! For me!!*

(Another explosion. On tape, a few moments of a stadium crowd cheering, along with a stadium crowd chanting, "Go-go-go". At the same time as the explosion, much of the furniture, excluding the desk, gets flipped over; plaster falls from the flies.)

*(*ANNABELLA *and* SMITTY *are obviously shaken.* COACH *has a hard time controlling his laughter.* CHARLIE *leans on the desk, panting.)*

ANNABELLA: *(Looking around at the furniture)* Did Charlie do that? Did he? *(Screams)* Did he?!!!!

SMITTY: Christ, I don't know. I don't know what's coming down no more. What current he's got himself plugged into. All I know is that he's gone far enough for me. *(Looking around)*

ANNABELLA: Smitty, he never mentioned shit like this. This ain't right. It ain't right. I mean, the whole room shook.

SMITTY: What do you think I've been saying!! *(Calms himself)* Okay. Somehow I'm gonna have to stop him before he does any permanent damage.

ANNABELLA: *(Screams) The whole god damn room was shaking!!*

SMITTY: *I know that! (To himself)* Now think. Think! Now I ain't about to do this by myself. Right. I doubt if I could even slow him down by myself. Yeh. But with a couple of other guys, I'll bet we could tie him the fuck down. I'll be back in a few minutes, Annabella. *(He exits.)*

ANNABELLA: Smitty!! *(Short pause. Trying to be strong, to get a hold of herself. She approaches* CHARLIE.*)* Charlie. Charlie? It's Annabella. I'm right here, guy. I'm right beside you.... See?... It's me.... *(Screams) It's me!!!!! (She turns away, unable to control herself, crying. She is no longer able to hear anything* CHARLIE *says.)*

COACH: What can I say, Charlie? What's left to say but you are holding them, son. You have got them all right. In the palms of your god damn hands.

CHARLIE: *(Own voice; exhausted)* I do?

COACH: Look for yourself.

CHARLIE: Look where?

COACH: Still with the jokes.

CHARLIE: I want to see them!

COACH: Then look!

(Bright lights or house lights up on the audience.)

*(*CHARLIE *covers his eyes and screams at the top of his lungs. Lights off the audience.)*

COACH: Ain't this gettin funnier by the minute, Charlie? What do you say, Charlie, you set to go? *(He puts his arm around* CHARLIE*'s shoulder)* You ready, son?

CHARLIE: *(Takes his hands off his eyes; other voices; he smiles.)* I roam....

COACH: *(Pats him on the back)* Good move. Good move. *(Moves away from* CHARLIE *to watch)*

CHARLIE: I roam along beaches and missile sights and skeleton-filled closets. I roam the far corners of the earth with that hungry and eager expression. I roam in the gutters and in the board rooms and in the breakfast nooks of the land. I roam down the halls of fame. Down the halls of Congress. Down the hall of mirrors. And I roam between second and third, digging out ground balls. Digging myself in for the duration.
I roam in order that I may consume. I consume. *(He laughs.)*

COACH: *(Applauding; sincere)* Bravo. Bravo. I knew you had it in you, son. Great, great move. "I consume." *(He laughs.)*

CHARLIE: *(Still other voice)* I consume the books, papers, pencils, the skies, the Marlboro crush-proof boxes, every imitation Beatle song every written, ever imitation John Ford movie ever made and the originals. I consume. I consume them all and repackage them under my label.

*(*COACH *is having a great time—smiling, chuckling.* CHARLIE *is also enjoying himself, beginning to really feel his power.)*

CHARLIE: I consume the New Left and the Old Left and the Far Right all in one breath. One swallow. I consume.
I consume every shitful act imaginable, every act of true love believable and sift out the hits from the flops. *I consume!*
I got the original gift of hype. No one else has it. I consume!
I consume without question. Without asking. I consume from sunup to sundown. And I consume while leaning against a lamppost in the dark of the night. Boo! I consume!
I strengthened my eyes so more would be seen. I sent up satellites so more would be witnessed. I learned to smell so more would be smelled. *Whatever I touch is real! It's true! I consume!!...*

*(*COACH *holds up his hand—stopping* CHARLIE *before he has reached his climax.* CHARLIE *stares out, smiling, anxious, almost rocking on his heels.)*

*(*SMITTY *enters, his face black from smoke, his clothes torn. He is in shock.)*

ANNABELLA: Smitty! What happened?!!

SMITTY: *(Hardly able to speak)* In the streets. I can't believe it. The streets. One second it was all okay. The whole goddamn block. *Fire!!! (Screams) Charlie!!!!!*

ANNABELLA: Fire? Where? What's on fire, Smitty?

SMITTY: *(Staring at* CHARLIE, *screams) Everything's on fire!!!! Charlie!!!!!*

*(*COACH, *who has been watching this, puts his hand down, cueing* CHARLIE, *who now finishes his beat.)*

CHARLIE: *I am nothing but what I consume!!! I confess it!!!!*

(Another explosion, very loud. Also, fire or the "impression" of fire. The crowd noise again, along with the chanting of "Go-go-go". Also, the chanting of "Go-go-go" in other languages, the shouting of "Olé", etc, as well as chants of "Charlie, Charlie, Charlie")

(At the explosion, ANNABELLA screams, SMITTY screams out, "CHARLIE!". They both collapse to the floor. CHARLIE and COACH ignore them.)

(Tape off)

(CHARLIE is now like another person, giggling, laughing, bouncing about like a fighter after a knockout who is ready for all comers.)

COACH: *(Obviously very proud, but also a little sad, he puts his arm around* CHARLIE.*)* You're a beaut, kid. An A-number-one beaut. You really are. *(Pats him on the back)* Come on, you don't need me no more. It's all yours now. It's yours. Just take it away.

(Tape on. It plays now for the remainder of the play, getting louder—that is, the crowd should be heard as getting more and more enthused, taken away.)

CHARLIE: In vain!

(COACH leads the "crowd" like a conductor.)

CHARLIE: In vain one looks for the winner in the winner's circle. In vain one seeks the forecast in the skies. In vain one looks for justice in the courts. Answers from the pundits. From the priests. From the scholars. In vain one looks for human interest among interesting people; for public opinion among the public. In vain!
Your search is in vain. In vain the effort is made to evade my gaze. Again and again the effort is made to escape my eyes and my senses. *But it is all in vain!!!! Shapes arise!!*

(Organ "charge" music—like that used at baseball games to get the team going—followed by all yelling "charge".)

CHARLIE: All murders, kidnappings, rapes, deaths, births, society marriages, job openings, wars, elections, coup d'etats flow *out of me! Out of me!!*
Richard Widmark and Mark Spitz are other names for *me!*
All stocks, bonds, devaluations, inflations are in me at this moment.
And all classics, religions, moral philosophies are in me too!
If I weren't alive and kicking, where would they all be? But for me!
Who would terrorize, skyjack, cure the incurable, and win Heisman trophies?
Who would burn the midnight oil over the Great American Novel?
And the Great American Dream?
Who would cry at funerals? At crash sights? Outside courthouses? And on small knolls on college campuses with arms stretched out, head thrown

back, kneeling, *and wail?!!!!!!*
Who?!!!!! But for me!! But for me!!!! I confess!!! Shapes arise!!

("Charge" music. COACH *picks up the chant of "Go-go-go".)*

CHARLIE: *And welcome!!!!*
Welcome all assassination attempts. All new Italian elections. All
last-minute game plans. All rare diseases. All dazzling photo-finishes.
Welcome! Welcome! Welcome! Welcome! Welcome!!!!!
Shapes arise!! I said, arise!!!!

(COACH *is laughing. "Charge" music. In the background, rumblings, tremors,
minor explosions. Crowd is very loud now.)*

(CHARLIE *is now completely confident, completely on top—even too much so, so
that he is appearing a bit monstrous.)*

CHARLIE: *Arise!!!!!*
I am on first base and third base and everything in between.
I am Hunter Thompson and Laurence Harvey and everything in between.
I am The Beatles and Wings and everything in between.
I am I F Stone and Max Frankel and everything in between.
I am "Firing Line" and "Sixty Minutes" and everything in between. *I am!*
Yes!
I am "Citizen Kane" and "It Happened One Night", "Monkey Business"
and "Psycho" and everything in between.
I am Jackson Pollack and Andrew Wyeth and everything in between. I am.
You can believe me.
I am the rain and the sun, the thoroughbred and the bastard, the book and
the movie based on the book!
I am the hard sell and the soft peddle. I am the front page. And I am the
comics. And I am the obituaries, and I am the births. I am the buyer, and
I am the seller. The consumer and the consumed. I am the one, and I am
the many!!
I am everything...in between!!!!!
I am! I am! I am it! I confess it! Me! Me!! Meeeeee! I said,
Meeeeeeeeeeeeeeeeeeeeeeeeeeeeeeeeeeeeee!!!!!!!!!!!!!!!

*(The last explosion. Also many distant explosions that fade out—the sense that all is
coming down. The lights flicker on and off. The crowd goes wild. Deafening cheers:
The chants ended with* CHARLIE's *last line.)*

(CHARLIE *is really enjoying himself, dancing around. Blood pours out of his mouth;
he tries to wipe it away.* COACH *has run up to him and gives him a big bear hug;*
CHARLIE's *attention, however, is on other things—in fact, on everything.
He continues to dance and begins mumbling or chanting something to himself.
Slowly these mumblings become audible: he is chanting "me me me me".
The crowd is telling him he has a right to be proud.)*

(COACH *has picked up a large flash camera, maybe from behind* CHARLIE's *desk.* COACH *waves and coaxes* CHARLIE *into a suitable position. Finally, there is* CHARLIE *bouncing/dancing in front of* COACH. *He slowly looks out into the audience and gives us all the all-familiar #1 sign.* COACH *snaps the picture. Blackout on the flash.*)

END OF PLAY

JUNGLE COUP

JUNGLE COUP was first produced at Playwrights Horizons (Robert Moss, Artistic Director, Jane Moss, Managing Director) on 22 June 1978 with the following cast and creative contributors:

HOPPER . . . . Michael Moriarty
MOTT . . . . Stephen Rowe
BELLOWS . . . . Jack R. Marks

Director . . . . Andre Ernotte
Set designer . . . . Heidi Landesman
Costume designer . . . . William Ivey Long
Lighting designer . . . . Paul Gallo
Sound designer . . . . David Rapkin
Stage manager . . . . Bonnie Panson

CHARACTERS

HOPPER, *a reporter*
MOTT, *his assistant*
BELLOWS, *another reporter*

Scene One

(A hut on the edge of a village near the heart of the African jungle)

(Center, a few wooden crates arranged to make a sort of desk. On this desk, a radio transmitter, which is put into operation by turning a crank. A small wicker chair, behind this desk, facing the audience)

(Up right, a large pile of crates)

(Ferns, palms, jungle flowers in pots about)

(Stage dark)

(Distant jungle sounds)

(Then the sound of the transmitter being cranked into operation)

(Lights fade up.)

(MOTT is seated in front of the transmitter, cranking. He wears earphones. Around his neck hang three cassette tape recorders. He wears a gun in a holster. He wears jungle fatigues, a safari hat.)

(Upstage, HOPPER paces. He is getting himself mentally "up," readying himself, thinking about what he is going to say. He wears a cream-colored suit.)

MOTT: *(Into the microphone of the transmitter)* Hello, Kinshasa? It's Mott. I said, it is Mott! Right. Can you hear me okay? Swell. Hold on. *(Turns to HOPPER)* I got them, Hopper. *(Into mic)* What? You're going to have to speak up. That's better. He's here. Hold on. *(To HOPPER, who continues to pace)* I got them. *(Into mic)* What? What do you think? The weather's been peachy, a mother-fucking dream. *(To HOPPER)* Did you hear me, Hopper? *(Into mic)* I wasn't talking to you. Just hold on, will you? Can you manage that? *(To HOPPER)* Hopper, they're hanging. *(Into mic)* I know you're waiting. *(To HOPPER)* Hopper, come on!

HOPPER: *(Very distant)* Is that Kinshasa, Mott?

MOTT: No, it's Atlantic City. Who the hell do you think it is?!

HOPPER: *(Turns to MOTT)* Then you better give me that.

MOTT: *(Handing him the mic)* Jesus, what's wrong with you?

HOPPER: You ready?

MOTT: You're damn right I'm ready. I've been ready.

HOPPER: *(He takes a few deep breaths, covers the mic with his hand.)* Good. *(A few more breaths)* Then let's boogie. Hit it!

(MOTT *pushes the "play" button on one of his recorders. Sound of distant gunfire is played.)*

HOPPER: *(Into mic)* All indicators in the past twenty-four hours point toward a massive offensive by the rebel P T F. This push, which at first appeared geared toward disruption of government supply lines between the province and the capital, has quickly grown into a spectacular all-out victory march as the scandal-ridden government forces beat a hasty retreat. The Communist-supplied P T F looks to be unstoppable at this time. They gain mile after mile with no major resistance in sight. Rumors abound here of massive desertions and defections within the government's ranks. *(He covers the mic; to MOTT.)* Okay?

(MOTT *gives him a "thumbs up".)*

HOPPER: *(Into mic)* Left unprotected, possibly doomed to take the full force of the progressing rebel army, are the hundreds of hamlets like this village of Huanga, which lie in the path of the guns and mortar. Left to somehow fend for themselves, are the so-called "civilians" of this war: those too old, too young, too feeble, or too maimed already; the children, the women, those innocent of this country's complicated politics. It is hard now for this reporter to imagine, as I look out my window at the one dusty road which is Huanga, that just months ago anything remotely resembling everyday life, common human transactions—of love, of birth, of work and pleasure—was taking place. *(He makes a face—he is not sure he liked that last bit.)* As I speak to you now, the rebel P T F's guns can be heard shelling a similar village less than five kilometers off. And I am not the only one who can hear that awful thunder. The question on the minds of all of us in Huanga is not "if" but "when" will our turn finally arrive. What once might have been described as a colorful jungle hamlet has in the space of days been transformed by twentieth-century tactical warfare. What was once idyllic, what was once order and peace and heritage, is now pain and confusion—helplessness and panic. *(He covers the mic; to MOTT)* Hit it.

MOTT: *(Confused)* Hit what?

HOPPER: The panic!

MOTT: But I don't have panic.

HOPPER: Shit.

MOTT: You should have told me you'd want panic.

HOPPER: *(Into mic)* But this is not the panic of screams, of cries, of shrieks— at least not yet—instead, as this reporter stares out his window, I can hear an even more awful sound: stillness, silence, the harsh emptiness of waiting, expecting, of fear; a silence which suffocates the heart and strangles hope. Listen for yourselves. Go ahead. *(Short pause)*

(HOPPER *looks at* MOTT *and points at* MOTT'*s gun.* MOTT *nods.)*

HOPPER: A silence broken only by the occasional gun shot—

(MOTT *has gone upstage; he shoots his gun.)*

HOPPER: —as a proud villager wastes his cattle. In my months here, I have become increasingly impressed by the determined nature of these people. And now, like the Russians before a Napoleon, the Sioux before a Custer, they are set to destroy what they have lived a lifetime to gain, to erase what their fathers before them lived to gain, rather than leave their invaders a speck of loot. *(He makes another face, shakes his head in disgust, puts his hand over the mic.)* Something's wrong. It doesn't feel like it's hitting.

MOTT: Sure it is.

HOPPER: *(Into mic)* To adequately grasp the heat of the situation here, one would have to be standing where I am now standing. Hearing what I am now hearing. Looking out my window and seeing into their faces. Their eyes. Words themselves do not do justice. *(Covering the mic)* I don't like this. It's boring!

(HOPPER *is getting more and more upset.* MOTT *is worried. Into mic)*

HOPPER: At first glance, you would find no anger, no resentment mapped across the faces. Hear no wails toward the sky. No beating of breasts. See no tension in a man's grip, in a woman's cheek, in a child's legs. But this, as with so many things in the jungle, is pure illusion. The grief is here, believe me. I've seen it. *(He covers the mic.)*

MOTT: Take it easy, Hopper.

HOPPER: *(Into mic)* Last night, a captured rebel soldier was brought blindfolded into Huanga. And the built-up anger was released with a vengeance. Old man, woman, child poured out of their huts into the road. A general rage seemed to grip the village. I watched from my window as first they taunted with threats, then teased with sharp sticks, and last they tortured this prisoner to death. One elderly man in particular caught my attention. I learned later his name was Bamunda. He was a refugee of a neighboring village and had been witness to his granddaughter's rape at the hands of these rebels. I watched the tight-lipped rage of this man as he wheeled a knife and disembowelled— *(Covering the mic, trying to control himself)* This sucks! *(Into mic)* The rebel's body now rots in the road no more than twenty feet from where I speak. Look. Just look for yourselves. Look into yourselves and try to imagine this awesome spectacle. *(Suddenly and violently, he slams the transmitter's switches off. He throws down his earphones in disgust.)*

MOTT: Hopper?

HOPPER: GOD DAMN IT, MOTT, WHY THE FUCK SHOULD THEY LOOK?!!!!!

(HOPPER *moves away from the transmitter,* MOTT *just watches him.*)

HOPPER: I wouldn't if I were them. I wouldn't walk across the street to look. Not from that stale...tired...emotionless hackneyed canned shit!! (*To* MOTT) Turn that fucking recorder off. It's obnoxious.

(MOTT *does.*)

HOPPER: What a lot of dead air. JUST WHAT THE FUCK IS WRONG WITH ME?!!!

MOTT: I thought it was going pretty smooth, Hopper.

HOPPER: (*Looks at* MOTT) Smooth?

MOTT: Yes.

HOPPER: (*Smiling*) Right. It was smooth all right, Mott. Jesus Christ, I thought you knew more than that! A GODDAMN NEWS STORY ISN'T SUPPOSED TO BE SMOOTH!!! (*Short pause. Calmer*) It's supposed to bristle. It's supposed to feel rough and have friction so they feel like they're right there, right in it, and so they'll beg to stay put, so they'll push and shove to remain there. It's supposed to grab them by the arm and throw them in a chair and tell them to sit still and listen. It's got to combust and explode and rage out of control until it gets the adrenaline churning, the guts tightening, the heart banging away at the ribs.

MOTT: I know that.

HOPPER: IT'S SUPPOSED TO GET THEIR ATTENTION!!!! That's first and foremost. You have to do that somehow, anyhow, the "how" doesn't matter. Give them a tragic story, a gruesome story, a happy story that makes them cry, a painful story that makes their skin crawl, give them a surprising and baffling story—but always always give them a colorful story! Or you won't move them, you won't touch them, you won't burn them up inside and grab them and then DAMN IT THEY WON'T LISTEN TO YOU! (*Pause.* HOPPER *looks exhausted. He has got the frustration out of his system.*)

MOTT: Hopper?

(HOPPER *doesn't respond.*)

MOTT: Hopper?

(HOPPER *turns to him.*)

MOTT: Hopper, why don't you take a break for a while. Go take a walk around the village. That story can wait. (*Pause.*)

HOPPER: (*Head down, he nods.*) Yes. (*He starts to exit.*)

MOTT: And while you're out, I'll look for the panic.

HOPPER: *(Turns back to* MOTT*)* The what?

MOTT: *(Pointing at his recorders)* The panic.

HOPPER: Oh, right. I could have really used panic. *(He exits.)*

MOTT: *(Deep sigh)* I hate it when he gets into one of these moods. I don't understand why he's so goddamn choosey. I can't wait to get the hell out of this jungle. *(Stands up, going to the crates)* Panic, where did I put that? *(The transmitter bleeps. He turns, hesitates, then goes back to the transmitter, cranks and picks up the mic. Into the mic)* Huanga. Mott here. Mott! Kinshasa? I hear you. What? Say that again? What do you mean it went dead? Jesus Christ, are you kidding?...You didn't get the whole story? You assholes are SO incompetent I can't believe it! No, there's not a damn thing wrong with our machine! What did you do, trip over the plug?!...He's gone. He's talking with the village leaders. I really don't believe this, Kinshasa. Look, we're not going to be penalized because you're idiots! We expect to be paid for the full story. Every goddamn line! He was brilliant. I never heard Hopper be better. I don't care—we're busting our asses out here in this jungle. Fine. If that's how you want it—we'll try the Associated Press. I'm sure they'd be more than happy to...*(Stops suddenly, whispers)* Quiet. I hear something. *(Yells)* Ahhhhh!!!!!!!! *(He shoots in the air. He yells into the distance.)* Get back! *(He shoots again.)* Hold him down. Quick, behind you! *(Shoots again)* Duck! Duck! *(Into the mic)* I don't know what's happening. *(He bangs on the transmitter, making the noise of a struggle. Into mic)* What? You'll pay for half the story? You have to be joking.... *(Into the distance)* He's got a knife! *(Groans into the mic)* Get a doctor! Doctor! I'll use my shirt as a bandage. *(Rips some material into the mic. Into mic)* He stabbed me in the arm. *(Into the distance)* Stop him, he's headed for the ammunition!!!! Stop!!!! *(Makes a sound of an explosion into the mic)* Get me a stretcher!!!!! *(Into mic)* What? I can't hear you? We're right in the middle of it! *(Makes ugly sounding groans into mic)* You'll pay for the *whole* story? Fine. *(Into the distance)* Bring that stretcher over here! *(Into mic)* I'll talk to you later. *(Screams)* Ahhhhhhhhh!!!!! *(Into mic)* Goodbye. *(Screams again)* Ahhhhhhhh!!!! *(Switches off the transmitter. Suddenly calm)* Now where did I put that panic? *(He goes back to the crates, takes out a shoebox full of cassettes and starts sorting through them.)* I should have labelled these fuckers better. *(He inserts one into a recorder. Plays it: sound of bombs being dropped from a high altitude. He stops it.)* Interesting. I didn't realize I had that. *(Plays another: sound of military tatoo—drums and bagpipes. Turns it off.)* No. *(Tries another: sound of stadium crowd chanting "GO GO GO". Stops it)* I'd be curious to see Hopper find a use for that out here. *(He digs around some more in the box.)* I'd swear I had it.

*(*BELLOWS *enters. He wears a cream-colored suit, Panama hat, he chews on a piece of grass. He takes only a few steps on, stops, smiles, watches* MOTT. MOTT *does not*

notice him. MOTT *tries another tape. This one is the panic he has been looking for. Sound of people running, screaming, yells of "Mommy", etc.)*

MOTT: That's it. That's the one. *(Tape plays.)* I remember this. (MOTT *gets into the panic. Moves his arms like he is running as he hears the sound of people running; ducks his head at the sound of an explosion.)* Scream. *(On tape: a scream)* Scream. *(On tape another scream)* Run. *(On tape, people running)* Run faster. *(They are running faster.)* Faster! *(Faster. He turns it off. Smiles)* This'll help. Hopper'll like this. I better mark it before it gets mixed up again. *(Turns, looking for a pen, he sees* BELLOWS. *He is shocked. Pause)*

BELLOWS: Thought you'd never notice me, Mott.

MOTT: Bellows. How the hell did you get here?

BELLOWS: *(Walking around, looking things over)* To tell you the truth, it wasn't all that easy. You want to see my mosquito bites? I've got one here on my feet that's the size of a softball.

(Starts to show him; MOTT *just stares.)*

BELLOWS: I guess you don't. *(Looking around)* They do dig up the most out-of-the-way beats to run these coups, don't they? Yes, don't mind if I do.

MOTT: What?

(BELLOWS *sits in the chair in front of the transmitter.)*

BELLOWS: What's the matter, Mott? You don't seem too pleased to see me.

MOTT: Sure I am, Bellows.

BELLOWS: I'll bet you are. I'll bet your little heart is just dancing. But why the fuck should you be? If I were walking in your shoes, Mott, I'd be pissed as hell to be sitting all alone on a page one and then BANG BANG BANG—you have company.

MOTT: It really isn't that big of a story, Bellows. Honest.

BELLOWS: Honest Injun? It's peanuts, I suppose. It's background. Well, you just tell that to my editors, because for some reason they think it's big enough to catch a lot of eye back home, and big enough to throw a lot of heat my way to get my ass the hell out here.

MOTT: Suit yourself, Bellows.

BELLOWS: My thoughts exactly. So where's the big shot?

MOTT: Hopper?

BELLOWS: Good guess.

MOTT: *(Looking where* HOPPER *exited)* He's...he's out. I mean, he's gone, Bellows.

BELLOWS: Of course.

MOTT: You just missed him. He took off this morning—bright and early. Has some interview with a rebel general or something. Real big deal, he said. He might be days. But if you wanted to try and catch up— do you have a map?

BELLOWS: Thank you for the offer, Mott. But I think I'll just pay the porter and stick around. *(He stands.)*

MOTT: But he could be weeks, Bellows.

BELLOWS: I thought you just said "days", Mott. And he left his transmitter behind? Hopper without a transmitter—that isn't even a reasonable thought. That wouldn't even be Hopper. As I said, I'll hang around. It's funny how even "weeks" can sometimes turn into "minutes." *(Starts to exit. Stops)* One more thing, Mott. How come things are so quiet around here? I was sort of expecting a good bit of racket. What is this, some sort of native holiday?

MOTT: Yes. You guessed it, Bellows. It's a holiday alright.

BELLOWS: *(Pleased for having figured it out)* Right. I thought so. *(He exits.)*

MOTT: Jesus Christ, he's all we need.

(HOPPER enters, smiling, calm, eyes almost glazed.)

HOPPER: Mott, were you ever right.

MOTT: I was right about what, Hopper?

HOPPER: Just look at me. *(Holds out his hand to show it isn't shaking)* I needed to breathe. I needed to relax and calm my nerves and quit fighting myself. I was thinking too much, Mott.

MOTT: *(Confused by the suddenness of this)* That's great, Hopper.

HOPPER: Now get me Kinshasa again.

MOTT: What?

HOPPER: This time I have shit planned out beforehand. Don't you see that was where I was going wrong. I was trying to *construct* the touch—not *present* one. I was plotting, not feeling. So nothing was coming off gut-level. Now I know better.

MOTT: Hopper, something's come up.

HOPPER: *(Ignoring him)* Did you find the panic?

MOTT: I did.

HOPPER: Good. Then let's stick it to them, Mott. Why aren't you cranking?

MOTT: Hopper, just listen to me for a second.

HOPPER: Listen to what? I'm sure the tape's just fine. Now quit wasting time and get me Kinshasa.

MOTT: Hopper, I didn't mean the tape.

HOPPER: CRANK, GODDAMNIT! GET ME KINSHASA!!!!

MOTT: Sure, Hopper.

(MOTT *goes to the transmitter. Cranks. Looks over to where* BELLOWS *exited.*)

HOPPER: What the hell is wrong with you? (*Calm again*) This time I'm going to move them alright. I'm going to touch them so they'll feel it in their chests and on the back of their necks. I'm going to get their guts strung so tight they'll be humming!

MOTT: (*Into mic*) Kinshasa? Mott. Yes. "Again." Speak up. Louder! You can hear me okay?

HOPPER: You got them?

MOTT: (*Into mic*) There's some interference. There. Now hold on.

HOPPER: I'm asking if you got them?

MOTT: (*Holds out the mic to* HOPPER) Yes. (*Pause*)

(HOPPER *just looks at the mic.*)

HOPPER: (*Finally taking it*) Good work.

(MOTT *stands and gets his recorders set, taking glances toward where* BELLOWS *exited.*)

HOPPER: (*Into mic, quietly*) Hello, Kinshasa? Hopper. (*Takes a deep breath*) The peace here has been shattered. This war has finally found its way to Huanga village. As I speak, the rebels are less than a kilometer off. And steadily approaching. The sounds of their guns has carried—one might even say, has *covered* this hamlet—and now lingers in the heat and grows louder, comes closer, too close for comfort, too close for anything resembling comfort, too steady to let pass by, too sudden not to be taken aback, be carried away, be pained and frightened. At this moment now, out of huts, out of the jungle, out of their neighbor's huts where they were visiting, out of a stream where they bathed, out of the blue almost, out of their thoughts, their sleep, daydreams, out of their minds nearly with surprise, without warning, without time, with fear, the villagers run. From their beds, tables, from their games, washing, from their work on the roofs, on the skins of animals, on this night's meal which is left to cook and cook and burn. From relaxing, from courting, and from memory or rumor or blind imagination or gut reaction or ready-made plan or whatever—whatever— that's all past now, all gone, goodbye, from that to this, in a matter of, seconds, in a manner so sudden it's hard to describe, hard to express, hard to get a handle on, a matter of life or death. From that to this.

(B*ELLOWS* enters with a knapsack and his transmitter. He sees H*OPPER.* M*OTT* immediately gestures to him to be quiet. He nods, sets down his things and watches. H*OPPER* does not see him.)

HOPPER: As I speak, I see an elder move cautiously about, organizing the evacuation. He pauses. Holds his head in his hands and screams. Then continues just as cautiously, just as matter-of-factly, with the same organizational skill. And I see faces now beginning to swell with tears, hearts already sinking, eyes still making the effort to blink away a nightmare. And I hear a mother shriek as another might talk—that is, incessantly, constantly, without breath or pause. And I see a child coughing in the dirt, staring at fast moving legs. And a kettle on the fire, boiling over—unwatched, unattended, uncared for, orphaned. All eyes I see appear whiter than that which is real. All eyes, larger and rounder than a half-dollar slug. From what once was to this. Politics, border disputes, ageless tribal jealousies, greed, copper mines, mineral deposits. All that. All that withstanding. This is still hard to understand. Hard to put one's finger on.

(B*ELLOWS* is confused. He mouths to M*OTT*: "What?")

HOPPER: I look out my window and see white bundles, piles of clothes, a radio, a lifetime's savings, a child's heritage from his father's father, a culture, the tools of a craft. All on backs, on heads, under arms, in carts, already ripped, tattered in flight, in fear, in running for cover, shelter, in running to nowhere in particular, but running just the same, running to keep from standing still and letting the pain take hold. To keep from feeling. To keep from understanding, and failing to understand, to comprehend this. This what? This panic. I see panic. PANIC!!!

(M*OTT* turns on the "panic"—at first soft, though gradually louder.)

HOPPER: Out my window. Only a few yards away, I see fear, everywhere there is fear—on faces, in the dirt, the heat, the lack of a breeze—of the known, of the unknown. A political fear for a few, a human fear for them all, a fear for survival, and of survival, of what survival might bring, might maim, might remember, might just throw into their laps I see clinched wrist, mouth, hand. A clenched child, wife, son, grandfather. A clinched hope. A clinched life. I see terror. I see terror. And panic. Right now. This is happening right now! RUN! RUN!

(B*ELLOWS* goes to the "window", looks out.)

HOPPER: Out of my window. In the village of Huanga. Through my window, I can smell it. Can't you? Smell this stench, the stench of "Why do we deserve this?" The stench of confusion, of bad luck. The stench of "This can't just happen!" The odor of sweat, tears, of wailings, of "WHERE'S MY CHILD" and "GOD PLEASE HELP ME!" Out my window, only yards away, I can taste a madness. Can't you? CAN'T YOU?!! A madness pushed,

driven out of the realm of madness. Taste it. GO AHEAD AND TASTE IT!!
A thick, a salty, impossible to swallow so that it sticks in the throat. A taste
of despair, of blight, of doom. DOOM! OUT THERE ONLY YARDS
AWAY!! No words, no words can describe, I'm convinced of that.
How could they? Words weren't meant to. Not something like. Of this scale.
What is going on here. I'm trying to portray, the feelings, the sensations,
the emotions running wild, out of control, out of their depth, running off
the edge, off at the mouth, foaming at the mouth, running in the wrong
direction, running amok, RUNNING RAMPANT!!! NO WORDS!! NO
WORDS!! JUST LOOK!!!!! *(Pause)*

BELLOWS: *(Whispering)* Mott???

MOTT: Sh-sh.

HOPPER: Gunfire: "crack!" "crack!" Snipers have taken aim, set themselves
up good. So it seems. So it's down to this. Have set as their marks—a yellow
shirt. A hit! A birthmark on the neck. A hit! A silver necklace around the
throat. A hit! A bandaged pair of glasses. BINGO! BINGO! And explosions!
BOOM! And screams! *(He screams.)* And FIRE! FIRE! "WATER!" Where's the
pump? Who's manning the goddamn pump?!! LOOK!!! Out my window I
see huts topple into flames, engulfed, convulsed. I see the road becoming
muddy, but that's not water, it's blood! I see eyes mouth, "SPARE ME!"
I see panic converged with panic. I see time running out, running low,
running into the road and wailing! LOOK! LOOK! From what to this. To
what? I see all that was up now down, collapsed, all that was inside now
worn on the sleeve, all that was soaked now parched, all that was smiling
now retching. I no longer see any reason but an instinct, a gut without its
shell, without skin, without clothes, bare AND BURNING ALIVE!! *(He
screams.)* LOOK!! LISTEN TO ME AND LOOK!!! *(Screams)* THIS IS CHAOS!!
IT'S CHAOS! THIS IS FLESH AND BLOOD CHAOS!!!!! *(Short pause. He is
exhausted, drained. Calmly)* This is James Hopper. For C B S News. In Huanga.

(HOPPER switches off the transmitter, turns, he sees BELLOWS, who is incredulous.)

(Blackout)

Scene Two

*(The same. Night. BELLOWS's transmitter is now set up on the crate, stage right.
Jungle sounds continue in the distance.)*

*(HOPPER and MOTT center. MOTT is packing a knapsack with cans and other
supplies. The transmitter is on the floor, straps have been attached for carrying.
HOPPER, now wearing a revolver, is looking over the map. Long pause)*

MOTT: Hopper, it's not that easy of a hike. If you'd just let me get you a
porter...

HOPPER: If I could wait for a porter, then I could fucking wait and go with you in the jeep. I just don't have that kind of time. *(Short pause)* What was the name of the village?

MOTT: Luchacha, Hopper.

HOPPER: How long do you think it'll take you to pack the supplies and truck it all to this Luchacha?

MOTT: I figure I'll be there in three days, Hopper.

HOPPER: Then I'll be there waiting for you.

(Pause)

MOTT: You know, you could always just cut Bellows in on this story. Once he gets over the shock, I'm sure he'd see all the advantages.

HOPPER: This story is mine, Mott. *(Looks over the map)* Quit pestering me and pack, it's going to be morning soon. *(Pause. Over the map)* Luchacha?

(MOTT nods. Pause)

HOPPER: You sure it's on this map?

(MOTT goes over to HOPPER, looks at the map, turns it around—he'd had it upside down.)

MOTT: There it is, Hopper. *(Going back to the cans)* Maybe I should pack provisions for five days—just to be safe.

HOPPER: Luchacha. It doesn't look that far to me. And that path doesn't look too bad.

MOTT: It doesn't have road signs, if that's what you mean.

(Pause)

HOPPER: *(Looks up)* You know what really upsets me, Mott?

MOTT: What?

HOPPER: It's that I was just beginning to get myself positioned. Look at the twists I could have chosen from: I could have brought the rebel army into Huanga. "Their boots crunching down the road. Their gun butts splintering the doors of tin shacks." I could have had myself captured. I could have escaped. I could have had political discussions with the rebel leaders. I could have been ransomed. Or tortured.

MOTT: You'll have to save all that for Luchacha now.

HOPPER: Right. *(He laughs to himself.)*

MOTT: What's so funny, Hopper?

HOPPER: I was thinking how I'd really like to see Bellow's face when he finds out I've moved the coup to this Luchacha. He going to be sitting here and transmitting that he's found Hopper and that there isn't any coup, and I'll be in this Luchacha reporting from the new front. His editors won't know what to believe.

MOTT: You think they'll believe you?

HOPPER: If they don't, they're out one hell of a story, aren't they?

MOTT: They'll believe you. *(Short pause)* All set, Hopper. *(Picks up the knapsack and transmitter)*

HOPPER: Then let's go, you can see me off.

(They start to go.)

HOPPER: Actually this could be kind of enjoyable, Mott. A nice hike through the countryside. I might even knock off a broadcast or two along the way— just to keep from going stale.

(They exit.)

(Pause)

(From behind the pile of crates, a match is struck. Smoke. BELLOWS walks out, smoking. He has heard everything.)

BELLOWS: Nice try, Hopper. You get an A for effort. But that's about all you will get, because try cranking up that transmitter without a battery. *(He opens his hand, and there is the battery from HOPPER's transmitter.)* You god damn fool, did you really think you'd get away with it? *(He sits in front of his transmitter, cranks it up. Puts on the earphones. Into the mic)* Hello, Kinshasa? Bellows here. Bellows. Right, I'm in Huanga. This morning. Sure, I've seen him. Where do you think I am right now? In his hut. Wait a second. I said, wait a.... Hold your horses, will you! I can't let it rip. I said, I can't let it rip, because there's nothing to let rip. *(Short pause)* That's better. Hold on and I'll tell you. It's simple. There is no story. You heard me. There is no story, because there is no coup. Are you still there? He made it all up. Hopper! I can't understand you when you talk that fast. I said he just made the whole damn coup up. Don't you think I know that? But that's his editor's problem, not mine. Yes, I'm positive. No, I'm not lost. I'm in Huanga, damn it!! *(Short pause)* No, I do not mean he's been exaggerating, I mean he made it up! I don't give a shit if that's hard to believe. Then you get your butt out here! *(He takes a cigarette out and starts to light it, stops.)* I'm sure my trip did cost a lot. But those are the breaks. *(Lights it)* What? That was me striking a match. I guess it could have sounded like a gunshot, but it wasn't, okay? Look, is it my goddamn fault if nobody's fighting? That's just what it sounds like you're saying. *(Short pause)* What do you mean, this will cause an accounting problem? I know I get paid by the broadcast, but damn it...! What? Check to see if you have what right? There is no fucking coup! Damn it, I spent two weeks getting my ass out here.... *(Short pause)* Look, the closest thing to a rebel I've seen is one god damn farmer with one god damn rifle herding one god damn goat! Now is that a coup! One farmer! One! One! Sure, there could be others. People do live here. I said, people do live here. I don't know how many others!!!! *(Short pause)* What?! I CAN' T SAY IF IT WAS A RUSSIAN RIFLE!!!!! (BELLOWS *throws down the earphones and walks away. We hear the voice on the line yelling and talking very fast. Bellows suddenly grabs his hat and throws it on the ground.)* Fuck! *(He goes back to the transmitter and sits. Into the mic)* It might have been a Chinese carbine. Chinese. Chinese! It jumped my mind. And the white guy with him. The white guy, he spoke French. I'm sure it was French. Was in the bushes. Maybe he was the lookout.

(Lights begin to fade.)

BELLOWS: I heard him say something about mercenaries. From Cuba maybe. Cuba. Do I have to spell it? I don't know how many. How does two hundred sound to you?

(Blackout)

Scene Three

(A path in the jungle. Jungle sounds are now a little louder, a little closer, than in the previous scenes.)

*(*HOPPER, *with knapsack and his transmitter. He fans himself with his hat.)*

HOPPER: It sure is hot out here. That sticky kind of hot too. That wet hot that's so stuffy. I wouldn't be surprised to see a bird trying to swim through this kind of air. I'm soaked myself already. *(Wipes his face; calls out)* Hey, how about turning on the air conditioning, okay? *(Laughs to himself)* Now there's a thought. Air conditioning in the jungle. But I must say, I wouldn't buck at an ocean breeze right about now. Not on your life. Stick my face toward that wind. Close my eyes. Open my shirt. *(Opens his shirt, closes his eyes)* Jesus, I could almost feel it there for a second. How long have I been out here so far? *(Checks his watch)* Seems a lot longer than that. But isn't that just the way? First half of a hike always seems to go on forever. You're counting the minutes and you're counting the steps. Then the last half comes, and you just don't know where the hell the time went to. That's the way, alright. Anyway, I have plenty of time. I'll be in that Luchacha before I know it. *(Looks around)* This looks as good a place as any to take that breather. Give my sweat the opportunity to run off. *(Starts to take off the knapsack and transmitter, stops)* Sh-sh! Listen. Yes, to that, Hopper. You hear that? You're damn right I do. Isn't that nice? *(Smiles. Listening, he takes his stuff off.)* I've been listening to those jungle sounds all morning. Nice to have something to hold your attention. Shit, they're a hell of a lot more pleasant than any car radio, that's for sure. *(Laughs to himself)* Really, I could listen to them rattle on all day. And I guess I'm going to do just that, right? *(Turns *back to his gear, sits)* Let's see what's packed for us, Hopper.*(Pause. He opens the knapsack, takes something out. Unwraps it. Then suddenly stops, stares out over the audience. Quietly)* I see this leopard. No more than, say, ten yards away. His body pretty much hidden by the brush. His eyes, they look like big holes of yellow. They're fastened to the base of a palm tree. Very still. Only his shoulder blades are moving. Up and down as he breathes. But wait a minute. What was that? I thought I heard something. A rustling in the top of that tree. You hear it? Listen. There. There! Did you hear that little squeal? Oh look, Jesus, it's a baby monkey up there. Pink face. Pink hands. He's picking a fruit. Or trying to. He's obviously having a rough time of it. Yanking it loose. Now he's got it. Hear him? Another squeal. Listen then. This time, I guess of pleasure. Here he comes, shinnying down the tree. He's down. Begins to walk a... The leopard! I forgot about the leopard! He's up! He darts! A FLASH! A SCREAM! SCREAM! *(Calm)* No. That's a dumb story. Face it, nature isn't your beat. *(Starts to eat; looks back into the knapsack)* Mott sure packed us a lot of crap.

(Pause. He stares again.)

HOPPER: I'm at the edge of a plain. I hear the sound of motor cars in the distance. At the moment, they're only specks on the horizon. But it's obvious the cars, Jeeps, I think, are coming this way. Who the hell could that be? *(Short pause)* What's that? Did you hear that? It sounds like something's up in that tree. Look. It's a native. He has a rifle. What we heard was him loading his gun. What the fuck is...? What's going on here? The Jeeps are much closer. The native is less than ten yards from where I stand. Though I don't think he's seen me. Oh, Jesus, that's the Prime Minister's seal on the first Jeep. That's right. I remember reading in the paper that he planned a hunting trip for today. And that's him alright. But who's the woman with him? His daughter? It could be his daughter. The Jeeps, there are three of them, are now what? One hundred meters off. I check the native. I check the Prime Minister, he's busy loading a hunting gun. Then "CRACK!" What was...? "CRACK!" Gunfire! The P M's head wrenches back. "CRACK!" Then back forward. Falls into his daughter's lap. BLOOD! BLOOD! *(To himself: calmly)* This isn't bad. *(Continues)* The native jumps from the tree. He can't get up! His leg is broken! From the fall. He crawls. He's scared. The bodyguards have surrounded the Prime Minister! Incredible! I'm but a few yards away! We are! Look! The Jeeps speed off. The daughter is screaming! She tries to climb onto the hood of the car. SCREAM! SHE'S SCREAMING HER HEAD OFF! BLOOD! BLOOD! ASSASSINATION!!!!! *(Pleased, reaching for the transmitter)* That really isn't bad. I think they'll really like that. *(Starts to crank; clearing his throat)* "Blood!" "Blood!" *(Cranking)* See what a little time in the jungle can do Hopper? A lot more pours out of you than *(Cranking, though nothing "catches")* sweat. Come on, baby. Am I doing this right? Come on. Come on. Catch. Hello? Kinshasa? Come on, friend. Don't start getting temperamental on me. Hello? I said, hello? *(Short pause)* Shit. Come on, I've got a story to get out! I said, come on! *(Stops cranking)* Jesus do I hate machines. I better leave it alone. Mott always said the fucker's got a mind of its own, now I see what he means. I guess you're just not in the mood, right? *(Short pause, he looks at the transmitter.)* I'll give it one more try. *(Clears his throat)* "Blood!" Okay. *(Cranks)* Hello? It's Hopper. Catch. Catch. COME ON, DAMN YOU, WORK!!!! *(Stops cranking)* Oh, what the hell.

I'll just have to remember it, that's all. And who knows, that broadcast might even get better if I sit on it a little longer. Anyway, there's no point in pissing myself sick over it. So—let's get our ass moving, I can't dilly-dally around here, waiting for a machine to change its mind. *(Stands, picks up the knapsack and transmitter)* You heavy fucker. State of the art, you're not. And don't forget that. *(He starts to go, stops.)* Hey, wait a minute. The map doesn't say anything about a fork in the path here. *(Takes out the map)* Must be something new. Let me see now. Which looks like the oldest path? That one. Right. I'll take that one. *(He exits right. As he exits, the jungle sounds become very loud. As he returns, they are cut back to as they were. He returns, scratching his head.)* No. That was the new one. That's the path I want to take. *(He exits left. Jungle sounds very loud again)*

(Blackout)

Scene Four

(In the jungle)

(Jungle sounds low again, though a bit louder than during the previous scene.)

(HOPPER, with knapsack and transmitter. He is sweating heard, breathing hard, a little more confused now.)

HOPPER: And I thought this was supposed to be a *wide* path! If it gets any skinnier there isn't going to be room for two feet side-to-side. And what am I going to do then? I'm going to have to skip my way through this jungle. *(Forces a smile)* Now that would be a picture. Bellows, I'm sure, would just love to get a snapshot of something like that. That fucker, if it weren't for him. Forget it. *(Looks around)* Think I'll pause here for a second. Catch my wind back. Jesus Christ, just listen to you. Sounds like you haven't ever walked a few miles before. Huff-puff. Huff-puff. Just sit down and catch your breath! Right. *(Takes off his gear)* Least one thing is for sure, Hopper— you went and picked the old path. No new path would be so overgrown as this one is. Yes. That's one thing. How long have I been hiking now? Seems like weeks. *(Looks at his watch; shakes it)* What the...? It isn't.... Must have hit it against something back there. I wound it, didn't I? Yes. That's a shame. I'm going to have to get it fixed when I get to this Luchacha place. Or maybe I'll have to send it off to the capital. That'll be a pain in the butt. To say

nothing about being charged an arm and a leg. Those crooks. Too bad I
can't charge it to Bellows. If it weren't for that fucker.... (*Starts to take a drink
from the canteen*) I sure hope Mott boiled this first. Last thing I need is a set of
cramps. (*He starts to drink, then stops.*)
You know, Hopper, Mott, he was sort of right about all this. Much as I hate
to admit it, he sort of was. This isn't the nice straight hike that I'd figured
on. What with all this heavy crap to lug. I was expecting to do a lot of
sightseeing, but I've been too occupied with lugging and keeping both eyes
on this little trail to catch much of shit. So it hasn't been as much fun as
maybe I thought. But do I have to tell Mott that? I'd never hear the end of it.
I couldn't walk ten feet to take a pee without him wanting to give me
directions. No. He doesn't have to know shit. I'll just be sitting on one of
those big chairs in this Luchacha. A cool drink in my hand. Rattling the ice.
And Mott, he'll come driving up and say, "Hey Hopper, how was the trip?
Not as easy as you thought, huh?" And Hopper'll say, "What trip? You
don't mean that little hike, do you? That was a breeze." Yeh, there'll be this
nice breeze too. So I'll have my hat off. Right. (*Pause as he "feels" the breeze*)
Yes. So Mott'll come driving up in the Jeep, and I'll just be looking real
relaxed, real collected—I've just taken a shower—and I'll say, "Where the
hell you been, Mott? I've been sitting here thinking about you. What'd you
do, go and get yourself lost?" (*Pause.* HOPPER *quickly changes his expression.
He becomes serious. Takes a few deep breaths to shake his worries, then forces
himself to stare out, "work on" another story.*) I see what in front of me? Let me
think. I see in the distance—okay—through some bushes, into a clearing,
over there. Right. Things are moving over there. Wiggling. Maybe just some
birds, but let's move a little bit closer. What's that smell in the air? Wait a
minute. This just may be a booby trap. We have to watch our step. Take it
slow. (*Short pause; he walks slowly.*) It's a bunch of dead bodies. A day or
so old. The movement was that of birds, all right. Picking away. Maybe
five—no, more like seven carcasses. Probably an ambush by the looks of
things. Though I don't see any guns. The others must have taken them.
Guns being a big commodity out here right now. It's funny, as I look at
these victims, it's funny how a few months of war can toughen one. Just
about five yards away is part of a human being. The part that's left. Or the
biggest remaining part. His head is over there aways. His hair caked with
bits of dried blood. A gruesome sight, sure. But war numbs one. I feel
nothing. The man's head has its mouth open. Could you say that the man
has his mouth open? That would sound strange. He looks old. Too old to
be a rebel or a government soldier, though I know they're taking them older
now. Maybe he got caught in a cross-fire. But why the hell did they have to
lop off his head? What does that prove? I don't know. I hear something
moving. To my left. There's a ditch over there. Again, we have to watch
our step—take things slow.

(*Short pause. Then he screams in shock, covers his mouth and tries to stifle the
scream.*)

HOPPER: OH, JESUS CHRIST! OH, MY GOD! I'm going to be sick. My stomach. I'm going to retch. *(Hardly able to talk—in shock)* In the ditch. You won't believe this. I can't. I don't know how many. I can't look long enough to count them! Maybe thirty. Maybe forty. But not soldiers. Not young men. Not even old men. BUT CHILDREN! WOMEN AND CHILDREN! GIRLS AND BABIES! Oh, Christ. What did I say about being numb? Can anyone ever be that numb? Okay. This is what it looks like. You ready? You better be. The women are naked. What's left of them. Clearly they've been raped. Raped and butchered. Or was it butchered then raped? Does it matter? There are just pieces. Limbs. Parts. An elderly woman. I think. One can only guess. Her...her breasts, they have been ripped off. Pulled off. Jesus! There are fingers stuck to legs. Legs stuck straight up out of the ground. Shoeless. And footless. There's a dead mother. Naked. They all are. A mother. She holds what is left of her...JUST THE HEAD! JUST THE HEAD! WHAT THE FUCK HAS HAPPENED HERE!! THESE ARE INNOCENT PEOPLE!!! *(He is in tears, choked up. Then, suddenly, he is calm for an instant, though excited; to himself.)* This is pretty nice stuff. *(Back to being choked up.)* Slowly, I guess, we can figure out what happened here At least we can try. That might help. Can we ever really do any more than just guess? A village was in the way, maybe. Accused of harboring a rebel or two, maybe. Or one or two from the other side, maybe. I don't know. Does it matter? Do you care? So everyone was just rounded up, corralled out here. Why here? Because there's a ditch, probably. And then they were beaten here. Then humiliated here. Then tortured, raped here. THEN BUTCHERED AND MASSACRED HERE! But why? Tell me, why? Would those who have done this, would they simply say, "Why not?" Let's hope not. Let's pray not. That I could not take. I can take the blood. I can take the intestines. The guts and rib cages spread around here. But THAT I COULD NOT TAKE. THAT I COULD NOT STOMACH. "Why not?" "WHY NOT?"!! BECAUSE!!! BECAUSE THESE ARE INNOCENT CHILDREN!!!!!! *(He relaxes, takes a few deep breaths, then takes a drink.)* Nice. Now if that doesn't pique them, if that doesn't stick to their ribs, I don't know what will. You are hot, Hopper. Definetely, you are hot. You are boiling over. Now let's get this one out *(Turns toward the transmitter and starts cranking)* Oh shit, I forgot. The fucker is playing dead on me. Now, I have to be doing something wrong. Let me think: Mott just cranks it up and... Hello? Hello? *(Cranks harder)* I SAID HELLO!! I DON'T CARE IF YOU'RE NOT IN THE MOOD?!! *(Stops cranking)* Okay. Have it your way. We'll just sit here and wait it out. I'm a patient man. Just holler when you're ready. I wouldn't want to pressure you. Just say when. *(Pause. He looks around, glances occasionally at the transmitter. It is obvious he is trying to control his anger.)* That's it! That is it! I'VE GOT A STORY TO GET OUT! *(He cranks harder, harder, then suddenly the crank breaks off in his hand. He goes into shock. He cannot fathom not having his transmitter. He tries to put the crank back on, but it won't go. He begins jamming it on. Forcing of his strength. He drops the crank. Pause. He looks around. Then he screams. Pause. He looks around again.)*

Can anybody hear me? I've got a story. It's a jim-dandy story. You'll like it. It'll excite you. It'll make your skin crawl. Your heart flutter? If that's what you want. Whatever you want. It doesn't matter to me. I just have to know that you're listening. Understand? That somebody is listening. Anybody. I'm not picky. Do you see? There's just no point if you're not. There's no reason. No sense. None. *(Yells)* PAY ATTENTION TO ME!!!!! *(He waits, but obviously there is no response. The jungle sounds grow very loud, sounding very much like gales of laughter. He turns behind him, toward the sounds. They fade back to the level they were at. He is still in shock.)* I think we've rested long enough, don't you, Hopper? Come on, we ought to press along. *(He picks up the transmitter and knapsack. He starts to exit, stops, looks at his watch.)* I don't remember hitting this on anything. *(He exits. Jungle sounds grow loud.)*

(Blackout)

Scene Five

(Deeper in the jungle)

(Jungle sounds continue.)

(HOPPER with transmitter, though without his knapsack now. He is tired, almost stumbling. His clothes are a bit tattered.)

HOPPER: *(Holding his side)* Goddamn cramps. *(Drops transmitter; looks around; wipes sweat off his forehead)* Now, let me think. I got to clear my head and think this thing out. Right. Okay, I'm thinking. The way I see it—pulling no punches now—the problem is—and this is hard to say, but, Hopper, it has got to be faced—the problem is that you, Hopper, that your stories, Hopper, up to now, they may have *sounded* fine to you, they may have sounded just swell, but, unfortunately, as it turns out, Hopper, they were not. No. They touched shit. They excited nobody. THEY WERE JUST BORING!!! *(He tries to calm himself.)* Okay. Okay. I know. But what's the point in getting all upset about it now. Come on, let's just get back to work.

(Jungle sounds up. He turns toward them. Sound down.)

HOPPER: I wish they'd quit all that squawking. I'm getting a headache. Wonder what the hell's got into them. Now, how about this? I'm lost in the jungle. Okay? That's a good setup. There's a lot I can do with that. And I stumble across—just by accident, by plain dumb luck, I guess it pays to get yourself lost once in a while. So I stumble across a tribal ceremony. God only knows what the hell it's for. I am, say, twenty yards away. Behind a bunch of bushes. I'll have to keep my voice down. I don't think they've noticed me yet, and we don't want to make them self-conscious. A number of young men, say, sixteen years old. Their faces all painted in colored stripes. I suppose that means something. And they're dancing around in a

big circle. Kicking up a lot of dirt. To one side of these kids, there is a group
of old men chanting—very low, deep, like a dirge, I would guess. And next
to them, there's one white-haired man with a headdress. He's beating at a
mammoth skin-covered drum. The skin of a hyena, perhaps. Let's listen in.
(Pause. He scratches his head; he is not too sure if he likes this one. Quietly) The
bells you are hearing are those worn on the ankles of some of the women
here. You've noticed, I'm sure, that they're keeping a separate beat from
that of the drum. Very interesting. As a matter of fact, the ceremony is quite
moving, don't you think? I'm certainly gripped by it, aren't you? Sh-sh. The
dancers are breaking their circle. Hasn't the drum beat quickened? Or am I
imagining that? You know how the mind can play tricks. There seems to be
something in the middle of...I can't quite make out what.... It looks like some
sort of animal.... Let's get.... *(Stunned and pained)* Oh, my God, IT'S A...!
(Out of the story, pissed off) No, that's dumb! Nobody's interested in cannibals
these days.

*(Pause. He puts his head in his hands. Jungle sounds, maybe only one bird here
getting out of hand, getting very loud. He turns toward the sound.)*

HOPPER: SHUT UP!!!! *(Upset, he stands, starts to pick up the transmitter, to get
set to exit. Stops, looks out)* Brother. This is incredible. Almost indescribable.
It's gorgeous. My heart's racing like crazy. What a natural what? Scene?
Monument? God's creation? It's spectacular. I don't think I have the words
to.... What do I say? I don't even know what to look at first. I want to look
at everything first. I didn't expect this. I didn't expect to walk up that hill
and find, to discover such a waterfall as this. I'm left speechless. Mine
are probably the first white man's eyes to have, to be here like this, to be
standing where I am standing, to be taking in what I'm taking in, and taking
it all to heart. You know how thrilling a particular sunset can be? Well
multiply that thrill by a thousand times, a hundred thousand times, and
you would begin to get the sensation, the inkling of what I am feeling and
witnessing, why my head is spinning, why my throat is bone dry, why my
eyes keep blinking. Jesus. The drop has to be a good mile at least. At the
very least. Without exaggeration. A drop into one very sizable bucket,
alright. There are rainbows, everywhere, rainbows crossing other rainbows,
rainbows faded and others gaining in intensity. Pastel rainbows. Oil
rainbows. Water-color rainbows. Rainbows you can't recreate. You can't
speak about. Words do not do justice. What can I say? *(Short pause, then
quietly, calmly)* I have jumped. And I'm falling. I fall though it feels more
like I'm in flight. The view spins in front of me. Out of its frame. Alive.
Breathing. I'm like the mist. What a way to relax! I'm on my back. On my
side. I roll around. I stretch out. I tumble. Dive. Spin. Try a cartwheel or two.
You should try this. I push my hair back out of my eyes so I won't miss a
moment. A second. An emotion. Jesus, JUST FEEL THIS! I sing. I crack my
knuckles. Look down. Go ahead. I can't quite make out....I have to get a
little closer. The bottom has gotten a little larger. I can almost pick things

out. I can point things out to you. But don't wait for me to tell you, look for yourself. Look. I'm too busy. I'm too relaxed just now. I can just about... the bottom. Just about touch the rocks. Almost there. I'm reaching. I'm stretching. I'm...

(He screams in pain. He has hit the rocks. Short pause. Suddenly MOTT *and* BELLOWS *hurry in.* HOPPER *looks up.)*

MOTT: There he is! Quick!

BELLOWS: He's alive. I don't believe it.

HOPPER: *(Confused)* Bellows?

BELLOWS: Get a stretcher.

MOTT: It'll take half a day to get a stretcher down into this gorge.

HOPPER: This gorge?

BELLOWS: *(Over him)* Just get one! He's bleeding!

HOPPER: I am?

MOTT: We saw you jump, Hopper.

HOPPER: You saw me...?

MOTT: I don't know how you survived. It's unbelievable.

BELLOWS: Will you get that goddamn stretcher!!!!

*(*MOTT *hurries off.)*

HOPPER: Since when have you cared anything about my health, Bellows? *(Looking over himself)* I'm bleeding...? *(To* BELLOWS*)* Why are you staring at me like that?

BELLOWS: Just try not to move, Hopper.

HOPPER: Oh, I see. So you've got me trapped, is that it? After all these years, finally Bellows gets one on Hopper. You've turned the tables, haven't you? Let me congratulate you, Bellows, you're cleverer than I thought.

*(*HOPPER *holds out his hand.* BELLOWS *doesn't shake it.)*

HOPPER: Okay, you win. So I guess it's time we collaborated, right? That is what you want, isn't it? Collaborate with Hopper?

BELLOWS: Collaborate?

HOPPER: I know I've been a bit ungenerous in the past, but that is the name of the game, Bellows. You know, Mott suggested that we team up on this story. Too bad I didn't listen to him, could have saved me this walk.

BELLOWS: There is no coup, Hopper.

HOPPER: You mean you've already told your editors?! Jesus Christ, was that stupid. But wait a minute, we can wire them back and say there was a mix up, that's no big problem.

BELLOWS: There's no story, Hopper.

HOPPER: Sure, right now there isn't, because I've been out in this silly jungle, but that doesn't stop the future possibilities. Actually, I was thinking we could...

BELLOWS: No, Hopper.

HOPPER: Bellows, I won't let you take this story away from me!

BELLOWS: It's over, Hopper.

HOPPER: Over?? Oh, *over. (Pause)* I see. You clever son of a bitch, what did you do, bring the President to meet with the rebel leaders; sign an agreement to have free and open elections in the new year; gradual transfer of powers, celebrations in the streets, rebels shooting off their guns, white settlers packing for England? Not bad, Bellows. I just hope for your sake you got a few features out of it.

(Pause)

BELLOWS: Hopper, there's no story. Your network has disowned you. They've filed criminal charges because of the money you've been paid.

HOPPER: What?

BELLOWS: Three investigators have been sent to Kinshasa to bring you back. There will be a trial.

HOPPER: But I'm Hopper.

BELLOWS: Your entire career is now being looked into. I think it is safe to say, Hopper, that you're ruined. Already you've become a laughingstock back home.

HOPPER: *(In a panic)* No!!!!

(He stands and grabs BELLOWS *by the collar, he doesn't fight.)*

HOPPER: Oh, my God. They can't do that. They can't be serious. I'll fight it. I'll come out swinging and expose those sons of bitches for what they are. I'll take the goddamn stand in my own defense and then, god damn it, we'll see who's ruined! *J'accuse! J'accuse!... (Short pause)* On second thought, maybe I won't fight at all. I could confess and get on my hands and knees and beg. I could look sheepish and pained and wipe tears away from my cheeks and ask for pity. I could get religion. I could write a book. I could go on the lecture circuit...(*Suddenly, he hurries to the transmitter and grabs the mic. Into the mic)* Which would interest you the most?!

*(*MOTT *has hurried in with a small box.)*

MOTT: Sit back.

HOPPER: *(Pointing to the box)* What's that?

MOTT: Makeup, Hopper. There's a camera crew on its way down the gorge. They saw you jump. Three hundred feet and still alive, that's news.

HOPPER: What do I need makeup for?

(BELLOWS has hurried out and soon returns with a bucket of water.)

MOTT: You're supposed to have been lost in the jungle.

HOPPER: I have been.

MOTT: *(Putting on the makeup)* You need cuts and mosquito bites.

HOPPER: I have cuts and mosquito bites.

BELLOWS: *(Returning)* Not enough.

MOTT: *(To BELLOWS)* Rip his clothes.

HOPPER: *(To BELLOWS)* Why are you ripping my clothes?

BELLOWS: So it looks like you've been lost in the jungle for days.

HOPPER: I have been lost in the jungle for days.

MOTT: It doesn't look it.

(BELLOWS takes the bucket and throws the water over HOPPER.)

HOPPER: Why did you do that?

BELLOWS: So it looks like you've been sweating.

HOPPER: I have been sweating.

MOTT: Shiver. You should have chills.

HOPPER: But I don't have chills.

BELLOWS: It'll look more real if you have chills.

HOPPER: But it is real.

BELLOWS: Shiver!!!!

(Long pause)

(Slowly, HOPPER begins to shiver.)

HOPPER: *(Shivering)* How's this?

(Blackout)

Scene Six

(The same as the previous scene)

(In the dark we hear thunder and rain.)

(As the lights comes up we see HOPPER *still holding the mic.)*

*(*MOTT *and* BELLOWS *gone)*

*(*HOPPER *is wet, his clothes are torn, there are cuts on his face, and he is shivering.)*

(Jungle sounds loud.)

(Long pause as HOPPER *waits for a reaction. He taps the mic.)*

HOPPER: Testing. *(Pause. He gets up and slowly begins to exit. As he does so, he carries the mic with him, pulling or ripping it out of the transmitter. He goes.)*

(Blackout)

Scene Seven

(The heart of the jungle)

(Gunshots off)

(Jungle sounds out, for the first time in the play)

*(*HOPPER *stumbles on, the mic in one hand and a smoking gun in the other.)*

HOPPER: *(Entering, to the "sounds")* Go ahead, you noisy fuckers! I'm ready for you! *(Looks around)* What's wrong? Cat got your tongues? Why aren't you CACKLING?!!! Go ahead and CACKLE!! Boy, you have got my goat now. CACKLE!! I'm waiting. I'm tapping my foot! SQUAWK! SQUAWK! HOOT! HOWL! Damn it. HOWL! HOWL! *(Screams)* HOWL!!!

(He shoots into the air; short pause. He looks around, turns his back to the audience and then with the mic in hand turns back to us. Into mic)

HOPPER: Ladies and gentlemen, I want to apologize for having wasted your time. I'm sorry. I didn't mean to do anything wrong. I can't help myself, I guess. I don't know what is wrong with me. *(Choked up, continues)* As I'm sure you've gathered by now, everything I have told you has been a lie. Every story, I have made up. I don't know why. Really. It's as if there were something in me that...*(Breaks down)* Excuse me. I didn't want to do that. *(Wipes away the tears)* I'm not asking for pity. Try to believe that, it's important to me. Help me. Help me. *(Crying)* I don't want to be like this. I hurt. And I'm lost. I don't want to beg and twist and lie just to get you to.... I'd much rather if we could just—you know—in an honest and straightforward.... Without any of this shit. I'm very ashamed of myself. *(Choking on his tears)* What is wrong with me?!! Will somebody tell me what is wrong with me?!!! *(Totally breaks down. Long pause as he cries)* Forgive me. I'm sorry. I really am. *(He goes. Immediately he comes back.)* Jesus Christ, what do you people want? That man was breaking down! Right here! Right before your eyes! Is there anything you haven't seen? *(Pause)* Okay. Look. Maybe I have been doing something wrong. That's possible. I can admit that. No point in hiding the fact. Maybe I have been going at this all wrong. Sure. Fine. So now we've got our wires somehow crossed. Well, that kind of thing can happen, correct? But so what? So what's the big deal? What's the point in panicking, correct? We can get the old ball rolling again, can't we? You're damn right we can. There. Now, don't we feel better? I do. *(Sighs, relaxes a bit)* Now. Now comes the difficult part. Believe me, this is going to be hard to say. *(Clears his throat)* Well—I guess I'll just spit it out—I am going to need your help. Now I know what you're thinking: "Why should we help that S O B who's been boring us to death." And I expected that. I will take the blame for that. No point in hiding it. And I can recognize the fact that I can no longer request from you to *actually* pay attention. I've already blown that. It's too bad, but I have. I *have* been boring. So there. Now the crunch. So you're asking yourselves, what kind of help does that guy want? Right? Believe me, I don't deserve much. I just need to know, say, if something *were* to touch a nerve in you, whatever, that you wouldn't completely—for whatever reason—that you wouldn't just count me, well, out. I need to know that there is still the chance, understand? I need you to be—is it too much to ask of you to be *potentially* listening? Okay? *(A big sigh of relief)* Thanks. That is a weight off my chest. Now let's go. *(He's excited, as if he has just received his second wind.)* Does anyone remember Amelia Earhart? Anyone? You've *heard* of her? That's good enough. Well, I've found Miss Earhart, and she has consented to take a few questions. Now, what can I get her to say that might be of interest to you? Go ahead. What might strike your fancy? What might tickle you pink? Think about it. The possibilities are limitless, aren't they? There's no rush. Take your time. How about the Lindbergh baby? I have got him cornered, and I think we just might get a few words. If we play our cards right. Well? Come on, folks. Just think about it. What about Howard Hughes's *real* will? Huh? The one the C I A has been keeping from us. Interested? Just a little? Just let me know. You just have to get me started.

(A little concerned by this lack of interest)

HOPPER: What about a Nazi war criminal? He's disguised as a sheep baron. What about Hitler himself for that matter? Did someone say something? Hit a nerve? No? What about a secret bomb shelter? Doesn't that pique your curiosity? It would mine. It certainly would pique mine. With a secret missile sight thrown in for good measure? How about Leonid Brezhnev? You don't really think he's dead, do you? He's in the same hospital wing

as is J F K Ironic, isn't it? Farfetched? All you have to do is ask. What about
a lost civilization? A lost continent? A lost race? A lost white woman in
the jungle? What about an erupting volcano? I could take color slides.
Prehistoric mammals that walk on their hind legs. That walk on three legs?
One leg? No? Am I getting warm? Just say the word, okay? *(A little more
nervous, itchy)* How about a nice U F O? That usually gathers a crowd.
Or Jackie Onassis? No? What the hell's the matter with you? How about
pygmies with poison darts? A championship boxing match? Quicksand and
mummies? Curses and witch doctors? Voodoo chants and English names
carved into ancient rubber trees? Huh? I'm waiting! What about Jimmy
Hoffa? No? Oh come now. *(Pause. He calms himself a bit, then puts on a big
smile.)* As we speak he's in hiding with Mary Jo Kopechne. Now that's a
story, isn't it? No? You're tough, you know that? *(Pause, a bit broken now)*
Look. All I need is a little clue. Feed me. Tell me what the hell you want.
My intentions are honorable. I'll see whatever the fuck you want me to see.
I'll see whatever's going to excite you. What tantalizes you. Moves and
touches you. What gets you hot under the collar. What makes your palms
sweat, your blood boil, your feet stomp, your mouth curl, smile, snarl, cry,
shriek, scream out. You just have to fill me in. See, you have to tell me
what you want. *(Calm again)* Okay. Stop me when something sounds good.
Now, don't worry about interrupting. Ready? Lakes. Any takers? Anyone
from the Sierra Club? Large lakes. Small lakes. Marshes. With. Without
mosquitos. No? Sand dunes. Mountains capped with snow. Great plains
which appear to sway in the wind. You're missing some stunning sights.
(Edgy again) Pools. Pools of fish. Pools of disease. Pools of blood. Still
nothing? Colors. Red. Brown. Violet. Orange. Nobody interested? I'm not
going too fast, am I? War. Now, come on. Wars of independence?
Lost wars? Ignored wars. Wars of profit. Of pettiness? Wars to gain a
foothold on the continent. That's a good one. I'd be interested in that if I
were you. Can I convince you? Wars which start where other wars left off?
Well? I'm waiting. I'm tapping my foot. There must be something!

(Getting very upset; thinking hard)

HOPPER: Sex! How the natives do it. I can take movies. Too gauche? I can
accept that. Bones? Science? Bones which support theories of evolution.
Or bones which don't. I don't care. Doesn't mean anything to me. Hunger!
Hunger should fascinate somebody! Starving children. Crippled children.
Children and their dogs? Old people who are still going strong? That's
always comforting. How about lepers? Anyone still interested in lepers?
Speak up. Lepers which will make you sick to your stomach? Make you
think? Make you feel healthy and glad to be alive? I don't believe this.
Am I close? Tell me. Religion! The death of God! The death of two gods?
Five gods? You have to tell me what you want!!!! *(Paces around, desperate)*
Okay. Let's get something straight, shall we? See, inside me, within me,
okay, are all these things. Great things, bad things, one-time things. They're

all here. All bunched together in here. All just sitting in here. And all you have to do is STICK YOUR GODDAMN HAND IN AND PULL ONE OUT! I don't give a shit what you choose. Why should I? No skin off my nose, understand? I have sounds. I have shapes. I have funny stories and class reunions, decadence and misery, tragedy and gossip. Here! More than you could shake a stick at. All seasoned to your taste, your size, your looks, your wants, NOW JUST CHOOSE! I HAVE EMOTIONS TOO! Believe it or not. I do. More happiness, more sadness, more humility and hatred and fear of the unknown, of heights, of water, of closets. I have them! I have them! So what do you want?! I have different shades of the same emotions. Good and bad emotions. Hungry and jealous emotions. But always, I promise you, I HAVE ALWAYS, ALWAYS COLORFUL EMOTIONS!! So now for the last time, for Christ's sake, I NEED YOUR HELP!!! CHOOSE!!!!!!! (*Pause.* HOPPER *looks around, confused and angry. "There's no reaction" is what he's thinking. He is in disbelief. He almost goes, but then suddenly gets an idea; he sort of smiles, he takes the mic and approaches the audience. Into mic)* I love you. (*He waits, no reaction. Into mic)* Fire. (*Again nothing. And again)* Panic! (*Again)* Touchdown! (*Again)* Marry me. (*Again)* Don't look! (*Again)* Why have you forsaken me?! (*Again)* Watch out! (*Again)* Blood! (*Again)* Help!! (*Again)* Pay attention! (*And again)* Scream?!!! (*Starts to go, stops, tries again. He looks up and around—nothing. He covers his head, and slowly sits—broken.)*

(*Pause*)

HOPPER: (*Suddenly he flinches, he turns to his right. Quietly)* I feel something touch my hand. I don't jump. I'm not scared. Why? I look down. A child of about six has reached for and grabbed ahold of my thumb. Who are you? What do you want? The child leads me by the thumb toward a crowd of native boys, which parts for us. I notice no faces except that of the face of the crowd, which stares at me. The child nods to tell me—everything is all right. I believe him. Why? As we sit on a bench I notice that the child has been gesturing for me to look straight ahead. I look. A number of boys are playing some type of native game. I am interested. I watch intensely as the crowd behind first begins to chatter, then to cheer and finally to yell its lungs out. One of the game players holds a stick, which has been carved thick at the top. Another holds a lopsided ball. The ball is thrown, the stick swung. I'm catching on; I find myself chattering away. I blend in. I hear the "crack" of the stick. Everyone stands. I stand too. I lift the child so he can stand on the bench. Everyone yells and everyone includes me too. I see the ball begin to sail off. Farther. Farther. Cutting quite a trail. Farther. The chatter has become a storm that is deafening. I am screaming myself hoarse. The ball is going. It is going. My arms are waving. My voice is lost in the crowd. It is going. Yes! Yes! It's a home run! A home run! I'VE DONE IT! I'VE DONE IT! The crowd is going crazy! I'VE DONE IT! They're dancing on their seats—the stands are vibrating! I've never really felt anything quite like this. I've never felt anything that could match, that could come close!

FEEL IT! I can't describe. Words would not do justice. You'd really have to be standing where I am standing, seeing what I am seeing, feeling what I am feeling—YOU DON'T KNOW WHAT YOU'RE MISSING! FEEL IT!!! I'VE DONE IT! This is the happiest moment of my life.

(Long pause. He puts down the mic.)

(Blackout)

Scene Eight

(A path in the jungle)

(Jungle sounds low now)

(HOPPER sits center—as he was at the end of scene seven. He is limp, distant. He stares at nothing.)

(Pause)

MOTT: *(Off)* Wait, I think I see some.... I think I see *him*. Hopper! Hopper! I see him! Come on.

BELLOWS: *(Off)* Where?

MOTT: *(Off)* It's him! Hurry up. Over there. Hopper! Hopper!

(HOPPER does not react. MOTT enters.)

MOTT: Oh, Christ. You're alive. We'd just about given up a couple of times. You're alive, I can't believe it!

(He goes to HOPPER, who doesn' t react. BELLOWS enters, carrying his transmitter.)

BELLOWS: How does he look? Is he wounded?

MOTT: We've been looking for weeks, Hopper. What the hell happened? You okay?

BELLOWS: They tortured him.

MOTT: What?

BELLOWS: The rebels tortured him.

MOTT: Jesus, who said shit about rebels? Shut up. He doesn't seem to hear me. He must be in some kind of shock.

BELLOWS: I'll bet you those mother-fuckers brainwashed him.

MOTT: I said, shut up! *(On his knees in front of* HOPPER*)* It's Mott, Hopper. Can you understand me? Do you recognize me? Don't try to speak, just shake your head. *(To* BELLOWS*)* Come on and give me a hand. We have to get him back, he probably hasn't eaten for days. *(To* HOPPER*)* Don't worry, Hopper, we'll get you home. You're alive, and that's all that counts.

HOPPER: Hopper is dead.

(*Pause*)

(MOTT *and* BELLOWS *are taken aback.*)

BELLOWS: What'd he say?

MOTT: He said that Hopper was dead.

BELLOWS: I don't understand.

MOTT: Sh-sh. Quiet.

HOPPER: (*Quietly*) The moment they picked Hopper off the field, it was obvious this wasn't a common injury. Not a busted leg. This wasn't going to go away. The stadium crowd, they knew it too. You could have heard a pin drop in that place. Sixty thousand people silent. As they lifted him up, he gave out one terrible scream after another. Then he just stopped screaming. And that chilled everyone. They set him on the sidelines, and a couple of doctors fussed over him. Took off his helmet, loosened his shoulder pads. That's about it. That's about all they could do. And the game, it just stopped. Nobody felt like playing, and nobody felt like watching them play either.

BELLOWS: (*To* MOTT) Does this make any sense to you?

HOPPER: They rolled him over on his back. Christ. I'll never forget that. It was difficult to look at him. Instinctively, you just wanted to turn away. But you couldn't.

MOTT: You are talking about Hopper, aren' t you?

HOPPER: Nobody else, Mott.

BELLOWS: He knows who you are.

HOPPER: Why shouldn't I, Bellows?

(*Pause*)

HOPPER: Around me, like a wave, the crowd sat down, all one motion, as if now just one body. I sat too. A woman near me kept biting at her nails. I watched her teeth. For the longest time I could not look at anything else. Then a hand, from nowhere it seemed, slowly reached around the head of this woman, and gently pressed the head to a shoulder. She did not resist. I noticed a lip. With small lines of water running down it. I followed these lines up. Up until I reached the eyes, where the lines of water stopped. Where they'd begun. Sometime here I heard a horn. The kind of horn you can buy at these stadiums. And in that air it sounded unreal. I watched a father reach down and calmly lift that horn out of his child's hands, and I watched him put a finger to his mouth and in a very, very quiet voice tell his son: "no". Then, I guess you could say "finally", all heads moved as one, all hands pressed together, all feet were pressed flat to the cement floor, all faces flushed, all veins in all necks tightened, while down on that field there was a convulsion. There was a jerk. Just one. A large glob of blood—black blood—retched out of Hopper's mouth. And we watched as his eyes stopped. His chest stop. And that was it. Watching Hopper like that, I remember thinking to myself that, when my time comes, that is just how I would like to go—with sixty thousand people watching me. *(Pause. He stands; pointing.)* Is that the way back?

MOTT: *(After a pause)* Yes.

(HOPPER *starts to exit.)*

MOTT: Just one question.

HOPPER: Yes.

MOTT: If Hopper is dead, then who are you?

HOPPER: *(He stops, turns back)* Nothing.

(HOPPER *exits, followed by* MOTT.*)*

BELLOWS: *(Watching them exit, shakes his head)* Those filthy savages. *(He cranks up his transmitter; speaks into mic.)* Hello, Kinshasa? Bellows. Clear the lines. Let's boogie! *(Clears his throat)* As I speak, less than a yard away, lies the tattered, skinny, unshaven frame of kidnapped American correspondent, James Hopper. He has been found alive. He has survived an ordeal which at the moment we can only speculate about. Here are the general facts: Thirty days ago, James Hopper is kidnapped by a rebel force. Probably an extremist faction. He is beaten, blindfolded, and drugged. Attempts are made to brainwash—unsuccessful. Through all this, he somehow survives. Then out of the blue, he is set free. Why? On whose order? You can imagine his thoughts. Uncertainty can be its own torture. He is simply cut loose to fend for himself in the jungle. Without food, water, or weapon. With only the instinct to "make it". And now today, just moments ago, no doubt one of the happiest moments of this man's life—there he was, looking up at me. His face puffed by insect bites. His clothes shredded and soaked, his frame shivering, the strain mapped across his face. I cannot describe all I felt. It was incredible. An incredibly emotional moment. This is Thomas Bellows. For A B C News. Somewhere in the jungle.

(Blackout)

END OF PLAY

THE KILLING OF YABLONSKI: SCENES OF INVOLVEMENT IN A CURRENT EVENT

THE KILLING OF YABLONSKI: SCENES OF INVOLVEMENT IN A CURRENT EVENT was first produced at PAF Playhouse (Jay Broad, Producer) on 10 February 1978. The cast and creative contributors were:

REPORTER . . . . .Richard Bey
DOCTOR B . . . . Joe Regalbuto
MISS K . . . . Elizabeth Parrish
MR A . . . . .Jon Polito
JOHN L, JR . . . . Michael Miller
JOCK YABLONSKI . . . . Jack Ramage
JOE . . . . Michael Miller
FIRST WAITRESS . . . . Elizabeth Parrish
SECOND WAITRESS . . . . Deborah Mayo
FIRST REPORTER . . . . .Jon Polito
SECOND REPORTER . . . . Joe Regalbuto
BUDDY . . . . Joe Regalbuto
CLAUDE EDWARD . . . . .Jon Polito
PAUL . . . . Michael Miller
MARGARET YABLONSKI . . . . Elizabeth Parrish
CHARLOTTE YABLONSKI . . . . Deborah Mayo

Director . . . . Peter Mark Schifter
Set designer . . . . John Arnone
Costume designer . . . . .William Ivey Long
Lighting designer . . . . Marc B Weiss
Sound designer . . . . Leslie A Deweerdt, Jr

A workshop of THE KILLING OF YABLONSKI: SCENES OF INVOLVEMENT IN A CURRENT EVENT was first presented by The Mark Taper Forum Lab in 1975, directed by John Dennis.

CHARACTERS & SETTING

REPORTER
REPORTER'S WIFE
DOCTOR B
MISS K
MR A
JOHN L, JR
JOCK YABLONSKI
MARGARET YABLONSKI
CHARLOTTE YABLONSKI
JOE
FIRST WAITRESS
SECOND WAITRESS
FIRST REPORTER
SECOND REPORTER
BUDDY
CLAUDE EDWARD
PAUL

PROLOGUE

(Curtain open as audience enters. Stage dark)

(Dim light. REPORTER *stands center. He breathes heavily. Stares left. Appears immobile)*

REPORTER: *(Pleading)* Wait!... What's the... What's the rush... Let's take our time... What's the goddamn... *Not yet! (Shouting) Not yet! Wait for me! For Christ's sake wait for me!! (His last shout turns into a piercing scream.)* Not yet!

(Gun shots, off left)

(Blackout)

CURTAIN

ACT ONE

(Projection on the curtain: "The Death of John L Lewis")

(In this act the characters sit or stand, facing the audience. Never acknowledging each other, they are each in their own environment.)

(Curtain parts. Stage dark. After a pause, large spot on REPORTER)

REPORTER: It began at John L Lewis' deathbed. Because it had to originate somewhere. That was the eleventh of June, 1969. And there were five witnesses at John L Lewis' bedside as he died. This has been verified by all the accounts in the newspapers and attested to by all but one of the witnesses. Miss K was the third witness I interviewed and the only one of the five that I met with more than once. In total, I had three interviews with her, all in Miss K's apartment, because, she felt, she could be more at ease there. She worried her stomach condition could have created an embarrassment had we met in a more public spot.

(Spot on DOCTOR B)

DOCTOR B: Young. Well, younger than I'd expected. Say about twenty-seven. The interview was in my office. My receptionist showed him in. No. I did not understand what he was after. The interviewer was intense. That you couldn't miss. He too was ill. He had a tape recorder tucked inside his briefcase. The microphone's cord, it skirted under one flap. It was buckled. There was a switch on the microphone, which he turned on as he introduced himself and off as we were interrupted and again when he left.

(Spot on MISS K)

MISS K: No. No surprise when he called. He was young. His sentences were long. And they were followed by his fingers. Because John L, Jr had told me about the interviewer, I knew that I must be on his list. Sensitive. That's what I want to call him. And that made it easier for me to talk. Yes. He had that briefcase. All three times he had it. And the microphone in one hand. Even when he caught the illness. Though I don't think he turned it on in the end. Sometimes he set it on a table.

REPORTER: By the end of the third Miss K interview, she was feeling a hundred percent better, the stomach gas completely gone, and for the first time since Lewis had died ("in my arms", Miss K during the first interview) she said, she could feel soft spots in her stomach.

MISS K: These are the facts. He showed me a photograph. That was the first interview. We had three. That's how many I needed. It was the West Frantfort Tragedy picture. I didn't know John then. We met in '55. He said he wanted to get this in focus and that I shouldn't skip anything.

(Spot on MR A*)*

MR A: "I was just sitting in a corner." That's all I said. Who could remember what corner? He said he needed to know, that it was all important. Also about Miss K. I said what everyone knew. That she hadn't been forgotten when Mr John L Lewis passed away.

REPORTER: "In my arms", Miss K during the first interview. This was reaffirmed by Dr B (witness four out of the possible five) who said he sat on the edge of the bed holding his patient's wrist. Dr B: forty (today; about thirty-five when watched Lewis die), five-foot-nine or -ten, thinning dark hair; he allowed smoking in his waiting room; athletic—had played tennis before his stomach condition and has talked longingly of returning to his game now that he too is a hundred percent better; his office: all the smells of a doctor's office.

DOCTOR B: I must say I couldn't help the young man much. I hadn't even been the patient's regular doctor. No. I can't say whether that disappointed him. I had just come back from tennis, was paged to go to Lewis' room. Walked in. Saw the patient in Miss K's arms. (I didn't know Miss K then.) Took the patient's wrist. And he died. I told him I thought I was sitting on the edge of the bed.

MISS K: The picture? I talked about it. Started talking then couldn't stop. Yes, I said, he, Lewis, had had such thick eyebrows. And, oh yes, he looked that heavy when I first met him. Whether this is what he wanted, I don't know. He just kept saying, "Keep focusing" or "It all matters."

REPORTER: Dr B on stomach gas: It occurs when undigested matter reaches the stomach or when large quantities of acidic liquids such as coffee are swallowed. Miss K is seated. Her arms tightly crossed over her stomach. I showed her the photograph.

MISS K: As I said, about twenty-six. Maybe five-nine. Brown hair, cut fairly short. Glasses—at the first interview only. Deep, very clear, green eyes. Yes. He is a smoker. Quiet. I thought he was sensitive: He chewed his nails. The interviewer introduced himself and handed me that photograph, saying, "Tell me whatever you want about this."

DOCTOR B: And I said the patient died of a stomach condition. I knew this at the time, or maybe I found it out from the patient's regular doctor. Yes. He was interested and kept saying, "Don't leave a thing out. It all matters." How I don't know.

REPORTER: The apartment certainly was grand. Mr A of the U M W (witness number two) had been right when he said, "Miss K had not been forgotten." Mr A sat in a chair at Lewis' bedside. The chair is in a corner of the room. Mr A: average height. Black hair. Maybe early forties. Like Lewis, a former miner, his father Welsh. A complete union faithful: "I don't even know why I was there," Mr A had said as an explanation for being in Lewis' room and for having watched him die. Mr A abstained from giving a verdict on the "Was Miss K holding Lewis in her arms" controversy. Back in the apartment: At the first interview, I show her a photograph.

MR A: I said I didn't even know Mr John L Lewis except from speeches and what I'd heard almost since I was born. No. That's true. I never actually met him. And it was just sort of an accident that I was there at all. They said somebody should be there. And that day it was my duty to bring the flowers. I was a symbol, I told the interviewer. Yes. He was interested in that and everything I said.

DOCTOR B: I already said he was young. Yes. I could identify him. I remember what he looks like. Well, we also talked about stomach gas. He said he needed a medical opinion. He was ill. Had gotten his stomach condition from the other four witnesses. Yes. He talked about them. He asked what I knew, which was again next to nothing.

MISS K: Why did I keep talking after the interviewer left? Because I had got a taste of what relief was like, and wanted more. With the young interviewer there while I talked about John L, the gaseous stomach of mine was being emptied. The pain going away, for the first time since his death. I noticed the connection.

REPORTER: Miss K, at the first interview: seated, her feet upon the chair, her arms crossed, a forty-five, a beautiful lanky (it seemed then, verified at the third interview), not a glossy but a weathered woman in the Kennedy women's style. Not at all how this interviewer imagines a union boss' widowed mistress.

MR A: No. I don't think it was ever a question of him believing me or not. I felt he just wanted to know what I had to say. Anything I could add, he said, would be important to him. I said I was there as a symbol of the U M W, and even though I'd watched Mr Lewis die, I still didn't know him. I brought flowers.

REPORTER: Miss K (first interview) said Lewis had died in her arms. Let me summarize her picture: Miss K sits at the head of the bed. She is holding Lewis with one arm around his shoulders. She wears a light summer-cotton dress, green, she thought, with a sparse print of soft reds and yellows. Dr B is holding the patient's wrist. Mr A sits in a corner holding flowers. John L Jr. stands six feet away from the bed, to the right of his dying father.

DOCTOR B: I had the stomach condition too. And yes. Lost it in the same way as did the other witnesses. I passed it on to the interviewer.

MISS K: Imagine my surprise when I felt that first release of stomach pressure. I didn't think it had to go anywhere. I thought I was just getting better. So when the interviewer arrived the second time, I was already talking about John, had been talking since he left the first time, and didn't make the connection until he left a second time that I needed this interviewer there to feel better.

REPORTER: Miss K (first interview): "John L had been steadily losing weight in his last year. When he died he was bony, sunken, weak. In my arms, his face was absolutely white." She thought he was wearing blue pajamas with a faded check design. This picture stands without contradiction.

DOCTOR B: That's right. He got it from me too. He knew it. I would have stopped, but no, he said, he had to know it all. Everything was important. He asked me how I got the stomach condition. I told him from Lewis. All of us there got it when he died.

MISS K: He was the one who kept saying, "Go on. I need to get this in focus." So I did.

(Spot on JOHN L, JR*)*

JOHN L, JR: Yes. That's a pretty good description of him. Though I don't think the interviewer was as sensitive as Miss K feels. He was quiet all right. But there's a big difference between being quiet and being sensitive. I thought he was confused. No. I don't know about what. I was standing to the right of Father. That's as you enter the room. Five or six feet away.

REPORTER: The second Miss K interview wasn't the first time I felt the pains. It was the first time that I took notice of them.

MISS K: No. I didn't want to hurt the interviewer. Even then he knew what was happening, he wouldn't let me stop. What I had to say, he said, was more important.

REPORTER: My first interview produced a similar result both in me and in my witness, John L, Jr. To start my investigation I flew to Minneapolis. Lewis' son seemed pale though very willing to talk. He said Miss K was standing. And, he thought, looking out the window. Mr A sat in a chair. Dr B, as has been verified, held the patient's wrist. I felt ill. From, I thought, the plane trip. John L, Jr stood to the right, six feet away.

DOCTOR B: Yes. I was all better when the interviewer left my office.

JOHN L, JR: No. I don't believe Miss K's holding-Father-in-her-arms story. I know her. I called her about the interviewer. He said he wanted to know exactly what happened. That he didn't want to overlook a thing. He wanted a focus. Yes. He had a tape recorder. I said, I was there, and Miss K, Mr A of the U M W, Doctor B, and C, father's chauffeur.

REPORTER: John L, Jr, a psychiatrist, the son of the famous man. Thinner than his father had been. White hair. About forty. Maybe five-foot-eleven.

JOHN L, JR: He showed me the West Frankfort Tragedy photograph. I said I knew little about that. I did not know father well. We rarely saw each other after mother died. That was 1942. The interviewer did not question this. He said, "Go on, tell me anything you think I should know." The interview lasted a short time. Yes. When he left I was cured. I don't know why.

MR A: I did remember who was there. Me. Miss K. Doctor B. John L, Jr and the chauffeur. The interviewer said that helped. No. Why should I have mentioned my stomach gas?

REPORTER: I carried the half-hour tape of John L, Jr back with me to Washington. Mr A of the U M W was witness number two. We met in a motel bar. He said he had only been a symbol of respect from the U M W. Mr A asked for carbonated water. He brought flowers. I had indigestion. As I did with John L, Jr, and later with Miss K, I show him a photograph. He identifies it. I want to know everything.

MR A: Yes. I felt better after the interview. It was all gone. But no. I had no idea that he caught it.

JOHN L, JR: I had traced my condition back to the day father died. I thought it was psychological. I didn't at first make the connection with the interviewer. He also wanted to know about the other witnesses. I know Miss K. I don't think I told him much.

MR A: I didn't know it was something you could catch.

MISS K: So by the end of interview number two, I not only had noticed a connection but had discovered the cause—to talk with the interviewer means to be relieved of the stomach condition. He asked about John L, Jr. I didn't know why he and his father didn't get along.

REPORTER: Mr A in the motel bar had nothing else to say. I felt worse. Next was the first Miss K interview. Followed by the second and the third.

MR A: Since you mention it, I think he did say he felt ill as he left. But, no, I made no connection. That's all I can say.

(Spot out on MR A*)*

MISS K: I felt I needed one more interview. I asked the interviewer back a third time. I had to tell him. He was trying to focus it all.

REPORTER: Miss K (second interview) did not vary her descriptions. I felt even this repetition should be kept in mind.

JOHN L, JR: He shook my hand. Said the plane trip had made him tired. And thanked me for my time. I was the one who called Miss K. I'm not sure why. I was feeling much better. I still don't see him as sensitive. No. No, that was the only time. Yes. I can come back.

(Spot out on JOHN L, JR)

REPORTER: The second Miss K interview. She is seated and talking. And did not stop talking even as I stood to leave. She described John L, Jr as distant.

DOCTOR B: He had already had a number of interviews. My receptionist showed him in. He said, as he held out his hand, "You are going to feel better." And I did.

MISS K: The third interview. I am standing. He takes a seat. There is no longer any mention of John. He wants only to discuss the passage of stomach pains. I told him what I had discovered. The tape recorder wasn't on. I was 100% better. No. That was the last time. You're welcome.

(Spot out on MISS K)

REPORTER: By now (the second Miss K interview) my gaseous stomach, unmistakable. Well, yes. The connection, I was making it. As I left. Then she phones again, "I need to see you." I returned. Ill. Knowing what I wanted to talk about. I don't have this on tape.

DOCTOR B: As I've said, the interviewer was young. He was ill. Intense. I was sitting on the edge of the bed. Whatever I could remember was important. He would not let me stop. I was cured when he left. You're welcome. *(Spot out on* DOCTOR B)

REPORTER: The last interview, Doctor B. In his office. Yes. I know that's only four. See, the fifth witness, C, Lewis' chauffeur never made our appointment. I have reason to believe he didn't need to. Because it appears that the chauffeur, he too found relief, because as I called to arrange our interview, I felt his gas too pass into this interviewer. I'm sorry. That's a fact I should not have left out. The Doctor B interview. It was in his office. The receptionist showed me in. I know I am bringing relief. "You will feel better." I tell him, I need to focus. He has a medical opinion—Lewis died of a stomach condition. "Please don't leave a thing out, it all matters." Doctor B had been on the edge of the bed. I held a microphone. Whatever he has to say is important. According to Doctor B—Miss K was holding Lewis in her arms. My stomach tight. Yes, he was sympathetic. He wants me to stop. He says I look young. I look intense. I stand a foot to Doctor B's right. Why do I continue when I understand the connection? Because it is all too important. Because I need to focus!

(Spot out on REPORTER)

END OF ACT ONE

ACT TWO

(Projection on the curtain: "Yablonski's Campaign For The Union's Presidency".)

(A piano center. REPORTER *throughout the act sits at the piano. As an accompanist, he punctuates both his talk and the action with appropriate atmospheric pieces on the piano. Next to him, a signboard, like those used to announce acts in vaudeville.)*

(Note: The direction "sign" refers to posters that are held up by either participants in the given scene, by someone who just walks on with the sign, or are flown down from the flies.)

(As the curtain parts, the REPORTER *is playing something rousing, something to suggest a campaign. After a moment he stops, reaches over to the sign board and flips over a card: "Yablonskis Learns Confidence". He continues to play, though now something slow and whimsical.)*

REPORTER: *(Playing)* In the beginning... *(Stops playing, shrugs)* It had to begin somewhere. *(Continues playing)* In the beginning, it was Nineteen Hundred and Sixty-Seven...or thereabouts...when with the United Mine Workers of America in sad disarray...when with that man of men, John L Lewis, himself deathly ill...when with "Tough" Tony Boyle now holding the reins as president of the union...it was at this time...when a fiery Washington lawyer, a man well known for his liberal causes, of the name Joseph Rauh... or simply "Joe" as he was called...approached a gritty vice president of the U M W by the name of Joseph Yablonski...or simply 'Jock' as he was known. Joe sensed that Jock had a growing concern about the union's management. That Jock might be itching for a fight. That Jock was probably fed up with playing second fiddle. That Jock had been pushed just too far. So Joe approached Jock. He chose his words carefully. He wished to present his suggestion in the best of all lights. Joe asked Jock...to take on 'Tough' Tony Boyle for the Union's Presidency. Just like that. But Jock had his doubts. He had his misgivings. Jock had his deep concerns. Jock just didn't know. Jock had no idea. Jock needed time to think.... Two years later, Joe had convinced Jock. And Jock made Joe promise to be his campaign manager.

*(*JOE *and* JOCK *enter, talking to each other.)*

JOCK: Jock...

JOE: I'm Joe. You're Jock.

JOCK: *(To* REPORTER*)* I'm Jock.

REPORTER: *(Pointing them out)* Joe...Jock...

JOCK: Joe...do you think we can win?

JOE: I hope so, Jock.

(JOE *and* JOCK *exit.*)

REPORTER: *(He plays)* There was much more still to be said. *(Pause as he plays)* In preparation for the coming campaign, Joe took Jock to his favorite tailor in Georgetown. Joe was after a more presidential look for Jock. Eventually, all agreed upon the dignity of navy blue. *(He plays.)* The time—it's now Nineteen Hundred and Sixty-Nine. The last seven months of that infamous decade.

(Sign: "Mayflower Hotel Ballroom". An arrow points out the direction.)

REPORTER: And Jock prepares to announce his candidacy in the Mayflower Hotel Ballroom. Joe had had his wedding reception there.

JOCK: *(Entering, putting on his new suit coat. He speaks to himself.)* Jock Yablonski...Jock Yablonski—candidate...Candidate Yablonski...Candidate Joseph Yablonski...President Yablonski!! *(He exits. Cheers offstage)*

REPORTER: Joe had told Jock to slowly loosen his tie as he spoke.

JOCK: *(Off)* ...dictatorial and decaying administration. *(Applause, off)* ...an abject follow-the-leader posture toward the coal industry. *(Applause, off)* ...the absolute disregard for the needs and desires of the working miner. What have they done about safety conditions in the mines? Nothing! *(Applause, cheering, off)*

(JOE *enters, whispers something to the* REPORTER.)

REPORTER: Jock and Joe had worked together on the speech. They could no longer remember who had written which lines.

JOCK: *(Off)* ...out of touch, and we the people are out of control. I plan to change all that. Let's get rid of the cheaters, the swindlers, the crooks, the corrupt and the corrupting, the out-and-out liars and double-crossers! *(Loud applause, cheering, off)*

REPORTER: Joe and Jock's speech was a great success. Reporters fought to ask Jock questions. One asked: *(To* JOCK *as he enters)* Hey, Jock, do you think you can win?

(JOCK *is startled.*)

REPORTER: Then remembering what Joe had said, Jock answered,

JOCK: I hope so, Jock.

(JOCK *and* JOE *exit and quickly reenter, sit down.* JOCK *begins to write in a notebook.)*

(The REPORTER *plays.)*

(Sign: "Exclusive Restaurant")

REPORTER: That night, Joe and Jock had dinner together. While they ate, they spoke about the campaign. They discussed broad issues and the smallest campaign details in the same breath. As they pooled their thoughts, the equal enchantments of Purpose and Potential could be read on their faces. Midway through the meal, both men agreed that their first step would be to make Jock's name a household word.

(REPORTER plays.)

(Two WAITRESSES enter.)

FIRST WAITRESS: Hey, Maria.

SECOND WAITRESS: What?

FIRST WAITRESS: You know who that is? *(Points toward JOCK)*

SECOND WAITRESS: No. Do you?

FIRST WAITRESS: No.

(WAITRESSES exit.)

REPORTER: But that would be a big job, Joe told Jock.

JOE: *(Looking over what JOE is writing)* Jock, you don't spell it with a "K".

REPORTER: Then Joe explained what 'charisma' means. Jock was interested and promised to work on it.

(REPORTER plays. JOE and JOCK stand up and begin to walk.)

(Sign: "A Street in Washington, D C")

REPORTER: On their way home, Joe and Jock stopped at a corner and continued to plan how they would win the election. Later, they shared a cab to save money for the campaign.

JOE: Jock...just remember one thing. A candidate is always confident.

JOCK: *(Writing it down)* Got it, Joe.

(JOE exits.)

REPORTER: Restless. Joe stayed up all night, digging through his law books. He wanted to find out how the law could help his friend, Jock, win the election.

(JOCK starts to exit. REPORTER calls to him.)

REPORTER: Hey, Jock! Over here!

JOCK: *(Turning, seeing REPORTER)* Oh, hi!

REPORTER: What ya been up to, pal?

JOCK: Me? I've been real busy. I'm running for union president.

REPORTER: Oh yeh? That's terrific.

JOCK: At first I didn't think I had much of a chance to win.

REPORTER: No?

JOCK: But now I think I just might pull it off.

REPORTER: Great. Got the ol' confidence, do ya? Well, see ya around.

JOCK: Yeh. Yeh. Take it easy. *(He exits.)*

(REPORTER *begins to play something rousing, stops, flips over a new sign: "Yablonski Excites the Press!" He continues to play, though something slower.)*

REPORTER: The time? It's now a month later. The eleventh of June, 1969. After seeking out just the right office to set up as campaign headquarters, Joe and Jock decorated it themselves, hoping that it would reflect their own interests and personalities.

(Sign: "Campaign Headquarters")

*(*JOE *and* JOCK *enter.)*

REPORTER: In the center of the office are two large desks facing each other. On Joe's desk, an Eskimo sculpture of a walrus. On Jock's, a Degas sculpture of a ballerina.

JOCK: Joe, you know, I just realized something.

JOE: *(Looking up from his papers, very busy)* Realized what, Jock?

REPORTER: In the past month, Jock had had many new experiences which he has tried hard to find a handle for.

JOCK: That the most difficult challenge for the political candidate is not to lose touch with his own soul.

JOE: You're right there, Jock.

*(*JOE *and* JOCK *go back to work)*

REPORTER: *(Playing)*Joe and Jock were putting in a long night. Time itself had been forgotten as they planned the strategy. Joe argued for stressing the awful conditions in the mines; Jock, for the corruption of union officials. Joe smoked. Jock did not. *(He picks up a telephone, which is either on the piano or in it.)* Ring. Ring...Ring. Ring...

*(*JOE *picks up a phone near him.)*

REPORTER: Joe broke the news to Jock. It would have been hard on Jock, if his friend had not been there.

(REPORTER *and* JOE *hang up.)*

JOE: Jock, guess what?

JOCK: What, Joe?

JOE: John L Lewis is dead.

REPORTER: The two friends stayed up the rest of the night trying to understand Jock's feelings.

(JOE *and* JOCK *exit.* REPORTER *plays.*)

(*Sign: "Outside on the Street"*)

(*Two* REPORTERS *enter.*)

(*Flip-side of sign: "Reporters Wait for Yablonski"—arrow pointing out the* REPORTERS)

FIRST REPORTER: I said to my editor, what are you sending me out there for? This Yablonski, he's got nothing going for him. He'll fall flat on his face.

SECOND REPORTER: Yeh. And what did your editor say?

FIRST REPORTER: He said, if he does—get pictures.

(REPORTER *plays some solemn entrance music.*)

(JOE *and* JOCK *enter.* JOCK *addresses the* REPORTERS.)

JOCK: I did not agree with everything John L Lewis said or did....

(JOE *hands* REPORTER *a note.*)

REPORTER: (*Reading:*) Joe and Jock had to work hard to find the right way, *le mot juste*, which could describe Jock's feelings.

JOCK: ...but I did agree with the man. No man has ever done as much for labor in this country. Forty years of union service which should now weigh on the heart of every miner, of every union man in the country. Today, I am deeply saddened.

(JOE *and Jock EXIT*)

REPORTER: Later, Joe asked for the original copy of the speech to frame for his law office. (*He plays.*)

(REPORTERS *walk to another section of the stage.*)

(*Sign: "A Coffee Shop"*)

REPORTER: Joe and Jock's speech aroused interest and curiosity in the press.

FIRST REPORTER: He's got something, that Yablonski. Inside him. He really had me going.

SECOND REPORTER: Yeh. I gotta admit, he moved me too. I had chills.

REPORTER: What kind of man was Jock Yablonski? What made him tick?

FIRST REPORTER: He reminded me of a middle-aged...what's-his-name.

(REPORTERS *quickly exit.*)

REPORTER: *(Playing)* Public interest in Jock had been aroused. Editors now assigned features on Jock's home for the Sunday supplement. Women reporters were told to interview Jock's wife or else. Jock was now asked his opinion of the space program.

JOCK: *(Off)* Great?

REPORTER: His thoughts on the coming World Series.

JOCK: *(Off)* It'll be great!

REPORTER: Flying around the country, setting up speaking dates and making arrangements for the campaign trips, Joe telegrammed Jock, "You've become popular Stop Lewis eulogy great success Stop". When Joe returned to Washington, he noticed a change in Jock. He felt his friend had set off a fire inside himself. *(He plays something rousing. Stops. Flips over a new sign: "Yablonski Excites the Little Man". Then he continues to play.)*

REPORTER: As the campaign progressed, Joe felt like a manager of a boxer in training. He was cautious about how much to encourage and prod his contender.

(JOE and JOCK enter. JOE holds a letter. Sign: "A Letter Arrives")

JOE: Jock, here, read this.

JOCK: *(Reading)* "Dear Mr Yablonski/ We watched you on television and yesterday we heard you talk in Wheeling. I like very much what you say. It gives me a nice feeling to know you wanta help miners. My husband is a miner. He speaks of you like you was his brother."

(Flip-side of sign: "Yablonski Begins to Cry.")

REPORTER: The letter writer went on to say how her father had died in the mines and she dreamed he spoke good of Jock. Joe and Jock left immediately for Wheeling.

(JOE and JOCK exit.)

(Sign: "A Mining Hamlet Outside Wheeling".)

REPORTER: *(Playing)* Joe and Jock soon found themselves in the parlor of a small farmhouse, being surrounded by the laughter and cries of children. For hours they lingered in silence, listening to the story of the letter writer.

(JOE and JOCK enter. Look back. Exit opposite.)

REPORTER: As they left, both men made promises to themselves that they never would forget the face of this miner's wife.

CHILD'S VOICE: *(Off)* Mama...who was that?

MOTHER'S VOICE: *(Off)* Sh-sh!

(REPORTER plays as JOE and JOCK enter again.)

REPORTER: Hey! Hello there, Jock!

JOCK: Hello.

REPORTER: Well, how's the campaign going these days?

JOCK: A private poll says I'm gaining and gaining fast.

REPORTER: That's terrific. Congratulations.

JOCK: Thanks.

REPORTER: See you around.

JOCK: Sure.

(JOE *draws* JOCK *aside.*)

JOE: Jock...I don't know how to put this, but, you know, Jock, you can't be so friendly with everyone you meet....

JOCK: What do you mean?

REPORTER: Then Joe brought up assassination. It has happened before. A real possibility. Joe tells Jock. Jock listened.

JOE: It's just that...you've become a big threat to some people.

REPORTER: Jock said he'd be careful.

(JOE *and* JOCK *exit.* REPORTER *plays something rousing. Stops. Flips over another sign: "Yablonski Remembers His Roots". Then continues*)

REPORTER: The time—the moment of moments, election night. Nineteen Hundred and Sixty-Nine. After voting in his hometown, Jock flew back to Washington. Joe showed him a poll which said they were ahead by one percent with twelve percent undecided.

(*Loud crowd cheers, whistles, etc—off*)

REPORTER: As a gesture to sentiment, Joe rented the Mayflower Hotel Ballroom for their election night headquarters. There, just a few months before...

(JOE *and* JOCK *enter.* JOCK *appears very distant.* REPORTER *hands* JOE *a note.*)

JOE: (*Reading*) "The political pundits say it will be neck and neck."

REPORTER: Jock and Joe expected something awful. They heard of violence in District 12. "That's it", they said. But the trouble was short-lived, and they heard of nothing else.

(*During the next speech, the* REPORTER *plays very sentimental music, which gets louder as* JOCK *goes on. Also, as* JOCK *speaks, more and more people come on stage to listen. To watch*)

JOCK: Joe...I am thinking of an old man who I worked with in mines. His name was Arthur, but we called him Lucky, because he wore a charm around his neck. Most miners have few valuable possessions—Lucky had but one: a solid-gold lucky charm which he said had been given to him by his father, who had himself gotten it from his father. Lucky planned to pass it on to his oldest son—when the time came. That good-luck piece never left him, it was always around his neck in the pits, catching and reflecting light down there. He kept it shined up real nice. One day, a mine shaft caved in, and Lucky died before we could reach him. We soon discovered that on that day he had left his good-luck charm in his locker. As I said, I had never known Lucky to be without it. Ever since then, I have often wondered whether Lucky died because he'd forgotten that charm, or whether he foresaw his death and so purposely left it behind to pass on to his son. I'll never know. *(Pause)* But I do know one thing. It's the Luckys, the Arthurs, of this world, that's who I want to fight for!!

(A big crowd of observers now. They all applaud. JOCK *looks around, wipes a tear from his eye. All exit.)*

REPORTER: But the applause soon turned into stunned silence as the returns came in. Jock had lost. But numbers were not enough, one needed to look on the faces of the followers to understand the depth of Jock and Joe's defeat. *(He plays.)* Putting on their best smiles, Joe and Jock stood up to leave the ballroom. They walked toward the exit. A crowd of well-wishers began to surge toward them. Then one man pushed through the crowd. He approaches Jock from behind. Jock can't see him. The man reaches, grabs at Jock's arm!!!

JOE: *(Off)* Jock!! Watch out!!

REPORTER: That man was in tears. *(He plays. Pause as he plays.)* Joe started his book the next day. He called it "The New Union Politics". He phoned Jock often for insights into this day or that speech. Joe was after a true account. At lunches, Jock would read Joe passages from his diary. Joe wanted his friend to write the preface, but Jock thought that would make the book criticized as too partisan. The two friends met a couple of times at parties in the next few weeks. They would stand in a corner and talk. The bond of friendship which had been given to them would not fade away.... What had Jock gained from the campaign? There was so much, he would say. There was satisfaction even in defeat. There was discovery, insights into human nature and its hopes.

(Fadeout)

END OF ACT TWO

ACT THREE

(Projection on curtain: "The Killings")

(Curtain parts. Stage dark. After a pause, bright light; REPORTER *stands center. He speaks to the audience.)*

REPORTER: This happened!!

(Music comes on and REPORTER *sings:)*

The Pepsodent smile prevents cancer.
Right Guard will kill your crabs.
I don't wanta hear you say ya got no help, babe,
'Cause that's been cured in the labs.

The ad promises every help
From your stress and strain.
This product will protect you
From the sun and the rain.
I don't wanta hear ya say ya got no help, babe,
'Cause it's right there in the ads.
I don't wanta hear ya got no help, babe,
'Cause that's been cured in the labs.

Nine out of ten doctors will agree
That my love for you is genuine.
Seven out of nine reverends will worry,
That my love for you is a mortal sin.
I don't wanta hear ya say ya got no help, babe,
'Cause it's right there in the ads.
I don't wanta hear ya got no help, babe,
'Cause that's been cured in the labs.

(Music over. BUDDY, CLAUDE EDWARD, *and* PAUL *have entered during the song, and now sit close together, appearing to be driving a car.)*

REPORTER: *(To audience)* No kidding. You can't get away from it. Because this is what happened. So I don't like it any more than you will, but it *is important*. It *all matters. We got to get this thing in focus!* Don't we? Of course. There's no getting around that. So let me tell you once. Twice. Three times. Until you too are sold. O K? Fair enough? *Are you ready? Hold on?*
But first you got to know why. Why. *Really!* Why are those three driving east? *Because it matters! Really!* It's because of the greasy-haired intruder. Not

real hair, of course! Pure plastic. *Plastic!* A poly-fibered dome he had made
for himself. No fooling. It looks real though. Take my word.
So-o-o he has pointed them three along this eastward latitude and not a
one's about to argue. And *that's because* it has already been demonstrated
to them how a head unplugged is not something nice. O K? Fair enough?
So-o-o the three men are drivin' without questions and still with their
psyches hooked up normal, while the foreign visitor has got two hands on
each of their throats to stop 'em from lookin' in the wrong direction. Yeh.

BUDDY: I'd been driving a Chevrolet for as long as I could remember.

CLAUDE EDWARD: They're good. Don't get me wrong.

PAUL: I won't put them down.

BUDDY: But there was this party where a neighbor said, "American Motors."
Just like that. Out of the blue.

ALL THREE: "American Motors."

REPORTER: *Drive it hard, man!* From the great wide spaces of Ohio into them
hills of Pennsylvania. Got it? That's where they're headed right now. But the
three men don't know it yet. Yes, that's right. They're just sittin' three in a
row, *cramped in the front seat like stiffs!* Not lookin' one way either left or right
but straight ahead, just wrinklin' their clothes getting bunched in like that.
What a shame. *And only one ashtray for all three.* What a shame. So-o-o Paul,
he's on the hump, and he's already been covered with butts, but he's not
allowed to brush 'em off. No. No. *That would be too-o-o much!*

CLAUDE EDWARD: *(Holding up a .38)* This .38-caliber is a correct gun.

PAUL: *(Holding up a rifle)* Long. Perhaps a bit awkward in a small room.
But truly extra-ordinary. The .30-caliber rifle has been around a long time.
In its own slow way, it has developed a rather fine reputation as an exciting
and intelligent weapon.

REPORTER: *Hey! Who is that foreign fella holding your heads like you were
turkeys?* I think he ought to tell you. 'Cause it's strange. Interesting.
He ought to pump it right into your three heads. No words. It goes
something like this: He is a moon man. A genuine samurai from that
yonder yellow crescent. Wait. Wait. He's channeling something. Listen.
Listen. You're on your way to kill the three Yablonskis.

BUDDY: You won't be stunned by Pennsylvania's green rolling country.
Not after you've seen its mountains, forests, lakes, and clear rivers.

KILLERS: You haven't lived until you've seen the Quaker State.

CLAUDE EDWARD: We've just crossed the state line and we're on our way to
shoot some people.

REPORTER: *Just you watch it, Buddy! I mean watch it! Phew. Wow. He almost drove off the highway. Isn't that something. But you see the galactic samurai, he was steering too. So no problem. No sweat. Now get this. Get this.*

(BUDDY *is whispering something to* PAUL.)

REPORTER: Buddy wants to know, who are the Yablonskis. No joke. Of course the moon man picks this up and this time he doesn't get angry and boy is that a switch! You see he's been briefed on human emotions and lets the front seat bend its head and take a good long swig of real Kentucky whiskey.

PAUL: *(Holding up bottle)* I'm spending New Year's Eve with a gun in one hand and a bottle of Wild Turkey in the other. Still 101 proof.

REPORTER: And! And he lets the front seat turn its head toward the river. Oh, that's because of the plan. That's the place. That's it. The guns got to be thrown into that river when you're done.

BUDDY: *(Staring at where the river might be)* Man's soul is a mighty river.

CLAUDE EDWARD: The Monongahela River—you want to go where it flows.

PAUL: The Monongahela in moonlight. Just one pleasant way to know you're in Pennsylvania.

(JOCK, MARGARET, *and* CHARLOTTE YABLONSKI *enter. They are in their kitchen.*)

REPORTER: Dota-dot-dot. 10:21 P M. December 31st, 1969. In the Yablonski kitchen, Clarksville, Pa. 15322. And it all comes down to this—can the Yablonskis get to sleep in time?
Dota-dot-dot. 10:24/ Jock is holding his stomach. Why? His wife Margaret wrinkles her face.

MARGARET: Jock, you look ill.

JOCK: It's my stomach. It feels bloated.

MARGARET: Now, Jock, I've told you not to eat so fast. What's the rush?

REPORTER: What's the rush? Dota-dot-dot. 10:25/ Everybody's in the kitchen. Just what do they think they're doing in there? Dota-dot-dot. 10:30/ Charlotte, the daughter, wipes her hands on her apron. Does she know?

CHARLOTTE: Dinner was terrific, Mom.

REPORTER: Dota-dot-dot. 10:32/ That Yablonski family wanders outside without any coats on.

(YABLONSKIS *wander "outside".*)

REPORTER: Why should they worry about catching cold? Jock: Ahhh! Deep breath. Fresh air. Is it cold enough to numb an unbelievable pain? Do they sense what's coming down?

JOCK: I find nothing more relaxing than watching a full moon.

MARGARET: You can put a camera almost anywhere out here and take a good picture.

REPORTER: Dota-dot-dot. 10:40/ Are they really going to stay up to watch the New Year come in? Will they make it?
Dota-dot-dot. 10:51/ Jock holds Margaret's hand and Charlotte's hand. The three Yablonskis look up into the blue sky.

JOCK: A lot of people have waited years for the Sixties to end.

MARGARET: It is only natural to want to bid America's violent decade goodbye within the quiet of nature. And western Pennsylvania is nice for that.

JOCK: But the real reason for seeking out nature's peace is to tell yourself that tomorrow will be quieter and the Seventies a great improvement on the past.

MARGARET: Enjoy the outdoors!

REPORTER: Dota-dot-dot. 10:54/ They can be found on the back porch. Can they feel what's coming down?
Dota-dot-dot. 10:59/ Charlotte points out the Big Dipper. Are they prepared? They may scream and they may shout.

(REPORTER *turns back to the* KILLERS.)

REPORTER: *There! There! Pull in there! That's where it's all gonna happen! (To audience)* Yeh. That's what you'd hear the moon man sayin' right now if you only understood his lingo. But Buddy, Paul, and Claude Edward, they're plugged in good and tight. No loose wires. All circuits working. So they're already doing what's in the foreign fella's brain. It passes that fast.

CLAUDE EDWARD: We cut the telephone lines with safety in mind.

PAUL: We envision a quiet place. Without intrusion.

(KILLERS *are now out of their car and preparing to enter the house.*)

REPORTER: *The program is finding its human expression!*

BUDDY: It's only natural to want to prevent escape. So we've slashed the tires of every car but our own.

REPORTER: *And it's selling good!*

CLAUDE EDWARD: A lot of people might not have thought of it.

PAUL: But we cut the telephone lines *and* slashed the tires.

REPORTER: a-Z a-Z a-Z a-Z a-Z a-Z. That's the moon man setting up the next program. 'Cause he's gonna stay in the car.

(REPORTER *turns his attention to* YABLONSKIS.)

REPORTER: Dota-dot-dot. 11:08/ Well, is it over yet? Are the three Yablonskis still outside? How they gonna feel if they're not asleep when it happens?

JOCK: I am watching the moon on the last day of 1969. And you know what? The old man up there is still smiling.

MARGARET: That doesn't come as a surprise to me. I've been watching the ol' guy smile for years.

JOCK: Remain optimistic. There is hope.

REPORTER: It is 11:15 P M.

MARGARET: We've seen the sun go down, watched the moon, have lived through this decade.

JOCK: We deserve a Scotch! *(He exits.)*

REPORTER: Within the hour, the Yablonskis will be blown apart. You've got my word on that.

(JOCK *enters with drinks.)*

REPORTER: Dota-dot-dot. 11:17/ Jock brings drinks. Has he made them strong enough?

JOCK: While drinking to the New Year, let us remember the old.

CHARLOTTE: *(To audience)* I am a social worker. Which means I get very involved with people who need help. Children. The disabled. The poor. The elderly. They need our help.

JOCK: The New Year is also a time for remembering.

REPORTER: Dota-dot-dot. 11:25/ It is coming down. Really. Yet there still is a choice—pain or no pain. Exactly what does it feel like to be shot at point-blank range in the back of the head?
Dota-dot-dot. 11:27/ Everyone swallows. Charlotte chews her ice.
Dota-dot-dot. 11:34/ Is the front door still closed? Has anyone else come in yet? Jock turns off the light in his study. Margaret takes the glasses into the kitchen. But are they alone?

(REPORTER *turns back to the* KILLERS.*)*

REPORTER: So. Where are we? We're back with the cosmic samurai, that's where! His eyes vibrating a-Z a-Z a-Z in the back seat of the American Motors Automobile, setting up alternative tracks, and the three boys! *The three boys!* Under the influence, *under the unfluence,* still holding a gun in one hand and the Kentucky whisky in the other, open the front door. a-Z a-Z a-Z, that's what this means now. No joke.

BUDDY: *(Beginning to enter the house)* It ain't easy earning entrance into a house.

CLAUDE EDWARD: No. It's no picnic finding your way.

PAUL: First, you learn the layout. And that takes time, planning. Then you have to put your knowledge to work.

BUDDY: Think about what you want to do. It pays off in the end.

REPORTER: Sh-sh-sh. You don't say nothin' now. You don't have a thought in your heads to say. Three big stiffs with guns. Danger. Big explosive danger.

(*Attention back to* YABLONSKIS)

CHARLOTTE: Call it a party?

MARGARET: My favorite get-together is with our family.

JOCK: At our home here in Clarksville, we have maintained one quality standard for the entire family.

REPORTER: Dota-dot-dot. 11:36 P M/ What time is it? Jock checks his watch. Why? That matters. *It's very important!* Does he know?

CHARLOTTE: Goodnight Dad.

MARGARET: Don't say "goodnight", say "pleasant dreams."

JOCK: Dreaming is America's inalienable right. Be optimistic.

(CHARLOTTE *exits; she is off to bed.* JOCK *and* MARGARET *stroll to their bedroom.*)

REPORTER: Dota-dot-dot. 11:40/ Why doesn't Jock check the front door? What does he know? *That's very important!* Are the killers at this very moment standing on the front porch? Jock and Margaret take the back steps to their bedroom. Charlotte is in her nightgown. Yes, she has closed her bedroom door behind her. Question: What are her last thoughts? Dota-dot-dot. 11:45/ In bed, relaxed, Charlotte falls asleep. Question: What was the last sound she heard?

(JOCK *and* MARGARET *now in their bedroom*)

MARGARET: Do you have to keep those guns in our bedroom?

JOCK: (*Polishing a gun*) Violent rural crime is increasing in America. It is every man's right to protect himself and his family.

REPORTER: Questions Do Jock and Margaret have any idea? Wouldn't you just love to know?
Dota-dot-dot. 11:55.

JOCK: (*Putting aside his gun; hugging Margaret*) How to find life's pleasures— sip a good drink, surround yourself with family, strike a small blow for the beauty of nature, and the comfort of king-size beds.

(JOCK *and* MARGARET *exit, to bed.*)

REPORTER: Dota-dot-dot. 11:58/ The killers have started to climb the front steps.

(KILLERS *now in the house*)

REPORTER: Is that Charlotte's bedroom there? Are Jock and Margaret in that one? They want to know.
Dota-dot-dot. 11:59, December 31st, 1969/ The bedroom doors are pushed open. Jock's eyes are closed. Margaret's breathing is even. They are asleep. They are asleep. They made it. No pain. There will be no pain.

(*The* KILLERS *exit to the bedrooms. Immediately return.*)

CLAUDE EDWARD: At the appointed time, my gun wouldn't fire.

PAUL: Even the best plans can snag. Insure yourself against personal tragedy.

(*Music comes on.* REPORTER *sings,* KILLERS *do backup.*)

REPORTER: (*Singing*) Don't hate me, Mama.
Put down that big broad knife.
Oh, don't hate me, Mama.
Please don't take my life.
I ain't gonna think about my soul no more,
Once I get walkin' out that door.
I gotta run away, Mama, from them attitudes.
I gotta run away, Mama, from them attitudes.
I got the creative individual passion pink blues!
(And you better watch out, kids, or you'll get 'em too.)

(*Music off*)

REPORTER: So-o-o when the rifle wouldn't go off, now picture this, the moon man, he was jumpin' all over the back seat, bouncing up and down, *laughing! His eyes were laughin'!* I can't believe it. What's so funny? *What's so funny!* Huh? No problem. No problem. It's a test of the backup program. You understand, because Buddy, his gun *was* working, the mechanism will sell.

(BUDDY *exits.*)

REPORTER: So. Charlotte dead as a rock.

(BUDDY *returns.*)

BUDDY: (*Holding up his gun*) If the rifle doesn't work, we've got a pistol that will.

REPORTER: E-up E-up E-up E-up and *that* is moon jive for *kill! You understand.*

(KILLERS *have exited.*)

REPORTER: And Buddy, he's now killing Yablonski and his wife and his bedroom walls and floor.

(MARGARET *screams off.*)

REPORTER: Ooops. They're awake. Oh well. What a shame. *E-up E-up E-up E-up! Dead once. Twice. Three times. O-O-O-O-O-O more would just be too much?!!* Yeh.
No. You understand. No!!!! We guessed wrong. Because Claude Edward, his rifle, the moon man now unjams, and he takes as his target the back of Yablonski's killed head and shoots without aiming from maybe what? One inch away? You got it. *The coup de grace. You understand!!! So the place was really rocking!! I ain't kidding! The deed was done. It was sold!!! It happened!!!*

(KILLERS *return.*)

PAUL: Get away from crowds.

BUDDY: There are millions of miles of roads in Pennsylvania...

CLAUDE EDWARD: ...waiting. Just waiting.

(They get back in their car.)

REPORTER: *Dead one. Dead two! Dead three stiffs left back behind! What a show! What a show!* That's all the greasy lunar fella has left to say to the killers now back inside that American Motors Automobile and driving fast, singing off the car radio, and spittin' dust toward Cleveland, that is, Cleveland, Ohio.

KILLERS: We threw our guns into the Monongahela River on the first day of 1970.

REPORTER: Yeh. *I mean fast! Real fast!* You understand. Like you wouldn't believe. No joke. I mean, they were just a blur you'd get dizzy watching. They were getting away. Passing billboards which said—*It all matters! Get it in focus! It really happened!* And they're singing—all just one note now. Yeh. And then this moon man, you know, he begins to pull on the input plug, you understand...

(KILLERS *exit.*)

Oh brother, and he begins to short circuit his body, so there's just a smoke screen growin' around him. Coverin' him, you understand. And so before we get a chance to ask him who the hell he really was. See, he's spinning himself into a wave. Yeh, a wave. And he's already beaming off across space. Just a mystery. That's right, a mystery. No kidding.

(Blackout)

END OF ACT THREE

ACT FOUR

(Projection on the curtain: "The Interrogation of The Current Event")

(Curtain parts. REPORTER *center, in a smoky pool of light. He sits on a wooden swivel desk chair.)*

(He is exhausted, disheveled, unshaven; he smokes and drinks coffee throughout.)

(Pause)

(He sighs. He clicks on the Dictaphone.)

REPORTER: *(To audiences)* "How did I get them jokers to talk?" *(Smiles, almost snickers to himself)* Well, let me tell you, it weren't easy. I mean, it weren't no piece of cake, that's for sure. *(Smiles, almost snickers)* I mean, sure, yeh, I've had hard nuts to split before. But, nothing. And that is nothing with a big accent mark, that comes even close to this one. But at the same time, also nothin' quite as interestin' as this one too. As rich as this Yablonski thing. And nothin' quite as ugly as this either. As you'll soon see.
So I guess it's worth our while takin' our time. Worth then beginning from the top. Because...I don't know... I just sort of think this is a real important story to get out.
(Short pause. Lights a cigarette.)
Okay. I was in the Yablonski living room. Jock, for some reason, was keeping mum. Like a god damn steel trap, he was. And this reporter couldn't pry the time of day out of him. At least not yet.
And Margaret, what good was she? She'd lost her voice, by screaming for her life I suspect, so I knew there wasn't much of a chance of getting even a peep out of her.
So I was left at first with what? Don't have to be no genius to guess. I was left concentrating my efforts on Charlotte, the young Yablonski daughter....

*(Lights up right—*YABLONSKI *living room.* JOCK *stands in a corner, upset, tense, holding his head.* MARGARET *stands behind the couch, very tense, looking away.* CHARLOTTE *is on the couch, looking at the* REPORTER, *who has just swiveled his chair toward the living room.)*

CHARLOTTE: *(Confused, almost stunned, shaking her head. To* REPORTER*)* Well...
I guess you could say, it was just incredible. You know? I really don't have the faintest idea how painful it was, or even if it was painful at all. 'Cause, see as far as I can remember, there wasn't enough time for that. It was just, well, you know—unbelievable. There was this one moment when I felt like I was watching someone else, someone else like gasp for air. Someone else's

neck tighten, you know. It looked sort of like the head was almost about to be twisted off. I guess that was my head, wasn't it?

JOCK: *(Suddenly turns, explodes) Charlotte, I thought I told you not to say anything!!!!!!*

(Short pause, MARGARET *cries.)*

CHARLOTTE: I'm sorry. *(Short pause)* I just can't see what harm talking could do.

(Blackout on living room)

REPORTER: *(To audience)* This reporter began to feel like he was playing with something explosive. Something that could just go berserk in a sec. And I like that. That's hot. And it'll get hotter just as soon as the three Yablonskis break. Break wide open and their stories start erupting out. In all kind of colors. In all different sparks. Like a god damn volcano. Charlotte already was willing. And as for Jock, well, after the years I've put into this business, you soon learn how to read a guy, how to spot some fella who deep down inside wants to blab. Not just talk, but start blabbing out his gut. Start turning himself inside out. And deep down, I figured Jock Yablonski wanted nothin' more than just that. So it'll just take time. That's all. This joker, I told myself, ain't gonna stay mum forever...

(Lights on living room.)

(Pause)

(REPORTER *stares at* JOCK.*)*

REPORTER: *(To audience:)* There's an old trick in this business—that the more silence you throw at someone, the more uneasy they are gonna become, until pretty soon they're filling the silence themselves and spilling their guts just so they don't have to listen to no pin dropped.

(REPORTER *turns back to* JOCK.*)*

JOCK: *(Explodes/breaks) God damn you, I know you're waiting!!!* Jesus, haven't we already gone through enough hell? Haven't we? What the hell do you want from us? *For Christ's sake, leave us alone!!!? (He cries.)* Oh shit. Please. Please.

(Blackout on living room)

REPORTER: *(Snickers)* By this time, I figured, it wouldn't be long now. *(Short pause; lights a cigarette)* At this point in my search for what happened, I left the three Yablonskis to play upon themselves. And turned my attention to the three witnesses to the killings I had rounded up—not without some sweat. I'd made sure to keep these men separate—that's always a good practice.
I spoke with Buddy Martin first.

REPORTER: Go ahead, Buddy.

BUDDY: Well...you know, I'm not sure if this will be the kind of stuff you want, you understand, but, what the hell, here goes.
Well, I saw the girl when she was actually hit.

REPORTER: Charlotte?

BUDDY: Yeh, I guess. Hell, I don't know. And the first thing I noticed, see, was the loss of her nose. That's real clear to me. It was just gone, okay. *Vamos*. All of a sudden. How am I doin'?

REPORTER: And it left just a hole?

BUDDY: What? Oh yeh. Sort of a hole, I guess. Though there was still some stuff there where her nose had been. Yeh, and then her mouth. I noticed that a lot. See, it seemed to keep getting wider, you know. Like it was expanding almost, you know. Least that's how it looked. Her lips, I mean. But that's, I guess, 'cause of the blood which was coming out and speading. You know, *what* was blood and what was lips. It was hard to tell.

(Short pause)

REPORTER: Anything else?

BUDDY: Uh, well, it almost sounds funny now, but at the time, see, it really looked almost like she was talking. With her lips moving like that. And her throat moving. And her eyes were all of a sudden wide open. So for a second there, I thought she was talking.

REPORTER: But she didn't say anything.

BUDDY: No. It just looked like that.... Could I have a sip of that?

(REPORTER hands him his coffee.)

REPORTER: What about..? Wait a sec, I just lost the question. I had somethin' I wanted to ask. Oh, right. I remember. Yeh. What about color, Buddy? Say, patterns of color? Tones? Shades? You know. Talk to me for a minute about the color.

BUDDY: *(Takes another sip)* Color, huh? Well, there was red, of course. Mostly red, as a matter of fact. And...

REPORTER: And what? What else?

BUDDY: And there was some greenish thick stuff too.

REPORTER: Did the green get on her nightgown, Buddy? She had on a nightgown, right? Didn't she? Or was she nude?

BUDDY: No—a nightgown.

REPORTER: Okay. And so the green, it was thick?

(BUDDY nods.)

REPORTER: And did it get on her nightgown?

BUDDY: You mean, did it like splash on it?

(REPORTER *nods.*)

BUDDY: Yeh. Yeh. Now that you mention it. Yeh, on the shoulder, I think.
And. And in her hair too.

REPORTER: Her hair?

(BUDDY *nods.*)

REPORTER: Did it knot her hair, Buddy?

BUDDY: *(Thinking)* I'm not...no, wait a sec, yeh, it did. I'm sure of that.
I can picture that. Little clumps of knots, right.

REPORTER: *(Relaxes back in his chair)* Thanks, Buddy. That's a help....
Now, didn't you say you had something you wanted to show me?

(BUDDY *nods.*)

REPORTER: Great. Would you get it for me, please?

(BUDDY *exits, then returns with an oil painting—an abstract.*)

REPORTER: You did that? That's very nice. Could you hold it higher?
Mmmmm. Okay. Okay. I get it. What do you call it, Buddy?

BUDDY: "The Killings at Night".

REPORTER: Uh-huh. I can see that. Sure. It speaks, Buddy. It really speaks.
Thanks.

(*Blackout on* BUDDY.)

REPORTER: *(To audience)* At this point in time, I debated with myself whether
to move back to the Yablonskis, check how the hell those buggers were
holding up. I expected not too great. But instead I said to myself, "Shit, let
'em dangle a little longer. The more rope I give 'em...." You get the picture.
That sort of thing.
So I saw Claude Edward Vealy next instead.

(*Lights up on* CLAUDE EDWARD. *He is very nervous. He holds a brown paper bag.*)

REPORTER: Hey, how are you doin', fella? You're looking good.

(CLAUDE EDWARD *nods.*)

REPORTER: Hey, don't be nervous. I ain't gonna bite, for Christ's sake.
You want a butt?

(*He nods.* REPORTER *hands him a cigarette.*)

REPORTER: What's that on your chin? You growing something?

(REPORTER *smiles:* CLAUDE EDWARD *nods nervously.*)

REPORTER: They let you do that, do they? That's nice. That's real nice. Take a seat, Claude Edward. Stretch out. Don't worry about an ashtray. I never do. Someone will sweep 'em up.

(CLAUDE EDWARD *sits, drops his ashes on the floor though is hesitant about that.*)

REPORTER: So, tell me, pal, have you had a moment to think about my question?

CLAUDE EDWARD: *(Swallows)* Yes, sir, I have.

REPORTER: Good. Good. I really appreciate that. I'll bet a guy like you must be pretty damn busy, am I right? Got you playing all kinds of team sports, I'll bet, right?

CLAUDE EDWARD: Yes, sir.

REPORTER: Course they have. They'd be fools not to want a guy like you. Wouldn't they?

CLAUDE EDWARD: I don't know. I guess so.

REPORTER: Sure they would. Sure they would, shit. So—what do you say? You wanta just go ahead and plow in? You wanta just jump right the hell in? How does that sound to you? Okay? And me, I'll just be right here listening, okay? *(Short pause)* Go on. Go on. *(Short pause)*

CLAUDE EDWARD: *(Quietly)* I remember the smells.

REPORTER: What? A little louder, please.

CLAUDE EDWARD: I remember the smells.

REPORTER: Great. That's just great. Yeh, I'm interested in that. I'm with ya. Which smells?

CLAUDE EDWARD: Uh, hers. The older woman's.

REPORTER: Was hers the strongest? Is that what you're saying?

CLAUDE EDWARD: *(Uneasy)* Yes, sir, I guess so.

REPORTER: Go ahead. Keep going. Describe them.

CLAUDE EDWARD: There was. Uh. There was the smell of uh...of....

REPORTER: Yeh. Of what?

CLAUDE EDWARD: Don't tell me. It's on the tip of my tongue. Uh...sour milk?

REPORTER: Are you asking me or telling me, Claude Edward?

CLAUDE EDWARD: No. That's not right. Damn it. Don't tell me. I had it. I had it all described just a minute ago. I did.

REPORTER: I'm sure you did. I am sure you did.

CLAUDE EDWARD: It's of...you know...of... (*Suddenly explodes. Screams*) *I don't know!!!! I can't remember anymore!!!!* (*Covers his head, almost crying*) I'm sorry.

REPORTER: (*Relaxes in his chair*) Hey, you're doing just fine. Don't be so hard on yourself, fella. You're doing great. You're just a little nervous, that's all.

(CLAUDE EDWARD *looks up.*)

REPORTER: Here, take another cigarette.

(CLAUDE EDWARD *does.*)

REPORTER: And relax. Just settle back and relax, okay?

(CLAUDE EDWARD *nods.*)

REPORTER: Okay, let me ask you a few things. How 'bout that? Would you like that?

(CLAUDE EDWARD *nods.*)

REPORTER: Good. That-a-boy. Um, this smell, was it pretty thick? I mean, was it say so thick that you could almost taste it in the back of your throat?

(CLAUDE EDWARD *nods.*)

REPORTER: Uh-huh. Then if it's the kind of smell that I'm thinking of, I'll bet it stayed on your clothes for a while. Did it?

CLAUDE EDWARD: (*Swallows, wipes the tears away*) Yes, sir.

REPORTER: Stayed maybe for days?

CLAUDE EDWARD: Yes, sir.

REPORTER: Great. That's it. See, that wasn't so painful, now was it?... Now, wasn't there something you had to show me. I think you wrote me that, didn't you?

CLAUDE EDWARD: Yes, sir.

REPORTER: Is it in the bag?

CLAUDE EDWARD: Yes, sir.

REPORTER: Great. Well, then let's see it, okay? It isn't somethin' to eat, is it? I could do with a sandwich right about now.

CLAUDE EDWARD: (*Taking something out of the bag*) No, sir. It's a mobile.

REPORTER: A mobile? Why, will you look at that. Isn't that clever. And you made it, right? I mean you did all the work yourself, right?

CLAUDE EDWARD: Yes, sir.

REPORTER: That's just wonderful, Claude Edward. Those aren't sea shells, are they?

CLAUDE EDWARD: No, sir, they're chicken bones.

REPORTER: Chicken bones. Boy oh boy, that's great. Would you jiggle it for me. I'd love to hear how it sounds.

(CLAUDE EDWARD *does.*)

REPORTER: It's beautiful! Boy, who would have ever thought chicken bones could be made to sound like that. Do you have a name for your mobile, Claude Edward?

(CLAUDE EDWARD *shakes his head.*)

REPORTER: Right. It's just made to speak for itself. I get you. Well, thank you, Claude Edward. I really appreciate your having taken the time. Best of luck.

(*Blackout on* CLAUDE EDWARD)

(*Short pause*)

REPORTER: (*To audience*) Number three: Paul Gilly.

(*Lights up on* PAUL GILLY, *who holds a little ceramic bust in his hands.*)

PAUL: Well, you know, I guess you could say I remember faces the best. Some guys, well they can remember names, other guys can remember dates, I even knew this one guy who remembered shoe sizes. Ain't that odd? But you meet a lot of odd people running a restaurant. Come to think of it, I'll bet that's why I remember faces so good, 'cause I run a restaurant and I'm always behind the counter and that's about all I see of people, their faces, you know. I never thought of that before, but I'll bet that's why, what do you think?

REPORTER: Go on.

PAUL: Yeh. So as I was saying, when you asked me to think of what I remember, well, I'd have to say, it's the faces. it's mostly faces. Though not all three of them, 'cause you know I never did see the girl. She was Buddy's. But I'll bet he already told you that, right?

REPORTER: Go on.

PAUL: Yeh. So me and faces. Let me see. There was the old guy's. That's the one that really sticks in the head. His face. Or what was left of it, you know. But, you know, that's a real interesting problem right there, isn't it? I mean, even though there ain't much left, it's still technically called a face, am I right?

REPORTER: Keep going.

PAUL: Yeh. Well, let me think. Well, it wasn't so much that it was blown off. It was more like blown out, you know what I'm saying. From behind the head, see. So everything inside, all that stuff that's normally inside, it had come bursting out and pouring out or just sort of stringing out like rubber bands, you know, depending on what it is you're talking about. What stuff you mean. And it made—and this is real interesting I think—it made cracks across the forehead. You know how a piece of paper can get curled around the edges? Well, it looked something like that, you know. The forehead skin did. Right here, see. *(Holds up bust, demonstrates where on the forehead)* Do you see? I call this thing "Busted Head". Do you get it? It's a bust, see. That's the name of this kind of thing. See? You do get it, don't you?

REPORTER: Anything else?

PAUL: Let me think... Now, I ain't all that sure what you're after. But I did notice something I thought pretty peculiar. There was this piece of I guess it was him. The old guy. Though maybe her. Like maybe a little bit of ear or maybe lip. I don't know. Even though I know faces, when it comes to pieces of faces, I can get just as confused as the next guy. But what made this interesting, see, was that it had stuck on their dresser. On the side of it. And it had obviously hit the dresser, slid down about, oh, six or seven inches, give or take an inch, and stopped and stuck. Just like that. Like it was defying gravity. Isn't that interesting? It's my guess that it stuck 'cause it'd dried all of a sudden. You know, it just stuck, slid and dried, you know. That's what I figure, what do you think?

(Blackout on PAUL*)*

(Pause)

REPORTER: *(To audience)* So there you have it. How I was spending my time by scraping together the few random facts my witnesses could come up with. And how at the same time I was allowing the tension in the Yablonski living room to build. To mount up to and including that point where they would just crack. Break. And start talking.
By this time I knew I was close, in fact, I could almost taste my success. But still I held back, didn't go for the money just yet, because I wasn't about to rush shit at this time. I wanted to be absolutely sure that not only were the Yablonskis ready, willing, and able, but also that they were desperate. So desperate, that they'd almost be wetting their pants.
So I had myself some dinner. Found some leftovers in the fridge. Sat myself down in front of the T V with a beer. Took my shoes off. Caught a nap. You get the picture. And just every now and then, when the mood struck, I'd peek my head into their living room and toss something off. You know, just something to prick. Something along the lines of...

(Lights up on the YABLONSKIS*)*

REPORTER: I heard it got knotted in her hair.

*(*YABLONSKIS *cover their ears. Blackout on them.)*

REPORTER: Or maybe...

(Lights up on YABLONSKIS*)*

REPORTER: No nose—I have a witness who is sure the nose went.

(CHARLOTTE screams.)

CHARLOTTE: Please, Dad. If you won't talk, then let me!! *Let me!!!*

JOCK: *Shut up, damn it!! Let me think!!!!*

(Blackout on the YABLONSKIS)

REPORTER: *(To audience)* You get the picture. Right? And then I'd turn away
and walk out. And, brother, *(He snickers.)* you could almost smell their
desperation. Yeh. You could. Without a doubt. I knew I had 'em now.
I had 'em good. They were just wiggling in front of me.
But still, yeh, I held off. Still I waited. I kept watching T V. I kept peeking in
every now and then with zingers like "A part of the lip or the ear?" Kept
catching little naps. Kept my profile very low. Kept myself from pushing,
from running in on them there and screaming, "Talk! Talk!" From taking
their son of a bitch heads and ramming them together. I did. I waited.
My impatience stayed in tow.
And then. Finally, it all paid off. Paid dividends. Big ones. Because, see,
by now it was beginning to dawn on them. More than just 'dawn', it was
smacking them across the face. That they no longer had a choice. That they
no longer had an opening. Had a way out. That they no longer could do
nothing but come to me! They had to come to me! *To me!!!! Listen!!!!!!!!*

(Lights up on YABLONSKIS)

JOCK: *(In tears, breaks)* Okay! Okay! Damn it! Damn it!

*(Short pause; CHARLOTTE tries to give JOCK her hand, he pushes it away.
He speaks slowly and painfully.)*

JOCK: *(To REPORTER)* Okay. I was asleep. I don't know what I was dreaming,
so don't ask me. Then I saw the revolver. That's all. Not the barrel really.
Not any one piece of the revolver. Just 'revolver'. You know, like in quotes.
So suddenly my first thought was to think the house must be on fire. Fire,
yeh. That's strange, isn't it? I guess maybe some problems with the wiring
were on my mind. I don't know. But anyway, fire was my first thought.
Then—shotgun. The one I kept next to our bed. So obviously I started
reaching for it. Lunging, actually. Yeh. And it felt like my whole body—just
one huge spring—one large inhale and exhale. Up/down. And Margaret, in
the background. Somewhere behind me screaming... *(Breaks down, sobbing)*

CHARLOTTE: Dad...

JOCK: Leave me alone!!! *(To REPORTERS)* I assume this is the kind of thing
you're after?

REPORTER: Keep going.

JOCK: Well, she was screaming. Okay. And then all of a sudden, well, I felt
breathless, you know. Do you know what that feels like, to be breathless?
Do you? It's not like being out of breath. Nothing like that. It's like, at least

in my case, it's like for one solid moment being unable to breathe. Being unable to do anything. Unable to wake up or to fall back asleep or to cover my eyes or to get my hands on that shot gun. *Do you know what that's like?!!!* Then I found myself. Yeh. That's an odd way of putting it, isn't it? "I found myself". Well, I did, half out of the bed, reaching, grasping, my feet all knotted in the sheets, and Margaret kicking. Or maybe just one kick, I can't be sure. But she kicked me on the side and I felt that bruise, you know, somehow I was concentrating on that bruise of all things. And it felt like it was spreading. My whole side felt hot, okay?
So there I am, unbalanced—in every conceivable way, believe me. And that's when I started to feel, don't ask me why, but to feel angry. *All of a sudden I was angry!!!* And I was bitter. I was enraged. All I wanted to do was start breaking stuff. My own stuff! Smashing things. Anything. I just wanted to hear things being destroyed. Yeh. And also, this is strange. Also, see, everything also at that time seemed incredibly breakable. You know? So fragile. Even the telephone cord. I saw that. And I remember saying to myself, if I were to bend that cord it would *snap in two!!* Everything! I wanted to smash everything!! Everything was breaking apart. Me! I was! My pajamas! My wife! My fingers! My nightstand! *Everything! Do you believe that? Nothing! Nothing was being spared! Nothing was left!!!! Nothing!!!!*

(Long pause. MARGARET *comforts* JOCK, *who is crying.)*

REPORTER: Is that it?

*(*JOCK *nods.)*

REPORTER: It took you long enough.

(Blackout on YABLONSKIS*)*

(Pause)

REPORTER: *(To the audience)* And that's how I did it.

(He lights a cigarette.)

(Blackout)

END OF ACT FOUR

ACT FIVE

(Projection on curtain: "The Trip Into The Current Event")

(Curtain parts. Light. Soft classical music. REPORTER *and his* WIFE *are seated. Each reading a book.* REPORTER *smokes a pipe. Pause)*

REPORTER: *(Looking up from his book)* Dear...what time do you have?

WIFE: Four P M.

REPORTER: Thanks.

(Short pause as they read)

REPORTER: Dear...what's the date?

WIFE: It's December 31st.

*(*REPORTER *nods. Short pause)*

REPORTER: Uh, what year is it?

WIFE: It's 1969.

REPORTER: Of course it is.

(Short pause as they read)

REPORTER: *(Erupting) Then it's time! It's happening! I mean tonight! You understand! It's coming down!* You follow me? Pack up our gear, baby, 'cause we're going on a trip. We're taking a fast ride into the eye of a *major thing!* Call up weather and see if it's in the stars for tonight. *We've been invited!!* Check out the papers and see how we should dress. But just don't forget one thing, baby—we don't got much time. So we better hurry. *I mean really hurry!!*

*(*WIFE *exits.* REPORTER *speaks to the audience.)*

REPORTER: That's me. I'm over there with the wife. She's coming too. To take pictures. 'Cause I'm not about to miss one damn thing! No way. Not on your life. Not when opportunity knocks. Not with such a turn of events. As this. As this is. Are you with me? Do you see what I'm saying? Do you understand what is happening?!!! Don't panic. Don't sweat. Let's keep our cool. Right. Yeh.
So the Yablonskis, where are they? Must be over here. *(He points off; then waves them on)* Hey, Jock! Margaret! Charlotte! You come on out and show yourselves, you hear!

(JOCK, MARGARET, *and* CHARLOTTE *enter.* REPORTER *shakes their hands, winks at them, etc.)*

REPORTER: And killers! Over here! Buddy! Paul! Claude Edward! Don't be shy! You all come out here too!

(KILLERS *enter.* REPORTER *shakes their hands, whispers with them, pats them on the back, etc.)*

REPORTER: That's better. The whole gang. Now we know where everybody is. Right? Okay. *(He turns back to the audience.)* Well, I've got seven hours and fifty-nine minutes to get from there to there. That's two hundred and thirty-four miles. Okay? We make the trip, get a picture of everything that's important. Don't leave a thing out. Get this thing into focus. And then go home and get some sleep. That's the plan. Any questions? Let's go.

(WIFE *returns with a Polaroid camera around her neck.* REPORTER *and* WIFE *sit in their car and start driving.)*

WIFE: I got the Polaroid here with me for the *present*. And a Nikon in the back seat for the *past tense*. Clic-clic-clic. The Nikon's got for its face a super wide-angle to make it all too big, a telephoto to bring it all *too close for comfort*. Both with silencers. And more filters than you could shake a stick at. Cheese! Clic-clic-clic! Plus-X and Tri-X—that's the film we'll expose to the elements. Okay? Black and white—so stark, artistic, realistic, is that black and white. For anything that moves we've got the Bolex 16 millimeter. No one can say we're not prepared. Clic-clic-clic! There's a portable darkroom to make the past happen fast too! Cheese!

REPORTER: I'm driving now and looking for an entrance, any entrance, onto the Pennsylvania Turnpike. 'Cause we're taking that west, you understand. West toward Clarksville, PA!
And there it is! Right in front of our face. Interstate 76. A lucky seven but with an unlucky six. 'Cause they add together to make thirteen. So that's a misfortune. Our misfortune. Yeh. But we ain't turning around now. No. No way.
This guy in the toll booth, he says, "You two crazy? Don't you know there's a blizzard going on?" I say, "Just give me my goddamn ticket, mister. It'll take more than snow to keep me down!"

(Lights up on the KILLERS *and* YABLONSKIS.*)*

CHARLOTTE: Mom, do you think the Reporter will make it?

MARGARET: I don't know, darling. You better ask your father.

CHARLOTTE: Dad...?

JOCK: Charlotte, we'll just have to wait and see.

PAUL: *(To* BUDDY *and* CLAUDE EDWARD*)* I couldn't exactly say no.
Now could I?

BUDDY: I *guess* not.

PAUL: So I said, "Pal, we'll wait. But if ya don't make it in time, well, ya can't blame us. We've done our part."

CLAUDE EDWARD: Right. The Reporter can't blame us.

(*Lights out on* KILLERS *and* YABLONSKIS)

REPORTER: The hum of the engine, that lulls me to thinking: "It's December 31st, 1969, and, buster, you ain't gonna be stumped this time."

WIFE: (*Looking over pictures she has just taken, and taking new pictures*) This snap's already sixty seconds old. Quick! Another minute and we'll have to toss it in the *past file! So: What's it saying to us now? This second!* Cheese! Clic-clic-clic! You're looking down at the Atlas road map. A reflection of the highway in the window. Where's the energy flow? That's what we got to look for. It's got to be here somewhere! Clic-clic-clic! If you draw a line from your right hand to the edge of the road map. The map to the rear-view mirror. The mirror to your headrest. We've got a perfect square. *Perfect!* Is that significant? Does it turn you on? *How will it all fit together?* Cheese!

REPORTER: The tune coming in over the radio, it makes me just have to tap out its beat on the accelerator. The guy to the right. You know who I mean. In the painted V W. We've got to watch out for him. He looks crazy. Crazy. 'Cause he's wavin'! He's recognized me! Next time I'm going incognito.

(*Lights up on* KILLERS *and* YABLONSKIS.)

MARGARET: (*To* PAUL. *They are looking through a recipe book.*) I made this one for Jock on our tenth anniversary.

PAUL: And he liked it, I guess.

MARGARET: Oh my word! Liked it! He couldn't get enough of it!

PAUL: Would you mind if I took this down. I've been looking for a good crepe recipe.

BUDDY: (*To* CHARLOTTE) So you like the Pirates, do you?

CHARLOTTE: Yeh. What's wrong with them? What are you, an Indian fan or something?

BUDDY: White Sox. White Sox all the way.

JOCK: (*To* CLAUDE EDWARD) Let me see that rifle.

(CLAUDE EDWARD *hands him his rifle.*)

JOCK: You know I used to be pretty good with one of these. (*He aims it.*) Bam! Bam! Bam! What did you kids do, leave this out in the rain?

(*Lights out on* KILLERS *and* YABLONSKIS)

WIFE: *(Again with pictures and taking pictures)* Take a good look at this shot! It strikes me as important. I'm getting a definite plus reaction. The contrast excellent. You are singing with the car radio. What does it mean? Cheese! Clic-clic-clic! Mouth—wide open. An oval. *Oval. Interesting.* That's tremendously interesting, because your shoulder there—it's an oval too and because the slight space, see it, between your right palm and the steering wheel—that too's an *oval shape! Amazing! Unbelievable? A coincidence?* Don't count on it. Cheese. Clic-clic-clic!

REPORTER: One hour of driving and we've already seen seven bad accidents, and seven's a lucky number, so I'm feeling pretty good. But my nerves, they're getting a bit raw and in my head, there are these visions which will not stay down. It would take nothing for the car to slip over the embankments, through the steel guardrail, sending us to a bloody death. On the windshield, the snow's hitting down so hard you can just feel the glass getting weaker; we ought to stop. To rest my head. I can no longer distinguish between the radio's songs and my screams. I can't hear anything. The snowplows seem like ambulances as they barrel past us, flashing their yellow and red lights. At any moment the backside of the car could jackknife, and everyone here inside would be turned over and probably die in the explosion. Every year, why is this, they seem to be making headlights brighter. Besides ambulances there are trucks the size of mountains that are playing with us. But I ain't about to fall for that kind of suicide. I can feel the grooves in our tires filling with ice and losing traction. Don't do that! The car ahead is slowing down. We're gonna skid! I got to turn the radio off.

(Lights on KILLERS *and* YABLONSKIS*)*

MARGARET: Now who would like a cup of coffee? Boys?

KILLERS: Count me in. Great. Sounds good. Thanks. Black.

MARGARET: Jock?

JOCK: None for me. It'd keep me awake.

*(*MARGARET *exits.)*

CLAUDE EDWARD: *(To* CHARLOTTE*)* Take Buddy there. He's incredible. That's about all he ever does.

BUDDY: Don't listen to him.

CLAUDE EDWARD: *(To* BUDDY*)* How many hours a day do you watch T V? Ten? Twelve?

BUDDY: That's not very funny.

CLAUDE EDWARD: Look at him! He's embarrassed!

PAUL: *(To* CHARLOTTE*)* What are your favorite programs, Charlotte?...Charlotte?

CHARLOTTE: I'm sorry. I was just thinking I wonder where the Reporter is right this second.

(Lights out on KILLERS *and* YABLONSKIS*)*

REPORTER: After what? Three, four hours? The snow has slowed us down to where we're crawlin' on our hands and knees. Is time passing us by? That's what I got to find out. So I call collect and hear the operator hesitating and then two 'beeps'. I'm not surprised someone is listening in. They answer on three rings. "How about an update," I ask. "No change," they say, "you still got 'til 11:59. *'Cause that's when it happens!"* Then I shout, "hang up", and throw the phone against a concrete wall. The car is stuck in the snow. I can't call a towtruck, 'cause you never know who they're working for. We push it out ourselves. One slight slip and the spiked tires would rip our legs apart. But by the time I count to seven—three times—we're safe and on the highway. Drivin' fast!

WIFE: *(As before)* Here's a shot I didn't let get away. You're laughing. Or are you yawning? Or are you screaming? Which impulse is it? Which one? Do we have to decide right now? Clic-clic-clic! Your right hand and the steering wheel are in motion—a blur. Nothing defined. Out of focus. Cheese! Outside—through the window, telephone poles. No, trees. No, crowds of people are passing by. *Also a a blur! Notice the connection. It's important. It matters! Cheese!*

(Lights up on KILLERS *and* YABLONSKIS. BUDDY *is walking around in front of the others. He is wiggling his behind as he walks. They are playing charades.)*

JOCK: Wiggle! Funny Wiggle!

PAUL: Twist!

OTHERS: No! Four letters.

CHARLOTTE: Walk!

MARGARET: Strut! Funny Strut!

CLAUDE EDWARD: Sexy! That's got four letters.

OTHERS: *(*BUDDY *is exasperated.)* Don't stop! Try something else! Sounds like...

*(*BUDDY *begins spinning around.)*

EVERYONE: Spin...turn...circle...revolve..."revolve"?...spin...we said that... twirl...dizzy...wait, that was it...dizzy?...no, twirl, *twirl!*

CHARLOTTE: Girl! "Funny Girl?"

BUDDY: That's it!

PAUL: I thought I said "girl".

JOCK: Who's got another one?

(Lights out on KILLERS *and* YABLONSKIS*)*

REPORTER: It's stopped snowing. The sun's melting the top layer of ice, making the roads all the more slick and hazardous. I'm extremely tired. As each gust of wind hits the side of the car, I feel thrown about like in space. I do not think we'll make it on time.

WIFE: *(As before)* This one here. It speaks. clic-clic-clic! But what does it say? *Energy buildup.* Your left arm extending so your watch is exposed. Numbers. Important numbers? But not in focus. That's too bad. *Really.* Cheese! Clic-clic-clic! You are looking at the camera—eyes, they've turned red. What do you want to say? *Is it important?* There is something on your mind—a light: a reflection of a headlight! Got it! Cheese! Clic-clic-clic! Detail: nose. Detail: hair line. Detail: map of your face. Curves. Contours. Cliffs. The steep inclines. The energy fields. *Plus and minus!* The currents. The waves. Got it. Got it. *It's all there! Documented!* All make connections! Everything in relation. All mean something. Alone and together. *Everything is important! Cheese!*

REPORTER: Out of the radio I hear "hurry hurry hurry" as we pass towns called: "Are you making it?" And now with less than forty minutes to go I can't help but feel how unlucky we've been. *If the highway hadn't added up to thirteen! There would still be enough time!* Earlier I'd tried to drive around the slickest spots but now they are everywhere so we can just hold tight. My hands are numb and no longer an extension of myself. I have to turn the radio off *or else we'll blow up!*

(Lights up on KILLERS *and* YABLONSKIS*)*

JOCK: O K. Do we have it?

EVERYONE: I think so.

JOCK: Paul, you start.

*(*PAUL *begins to sing the following round. Eventually everyone joins in.)*

I learned from a wise old rat,
That curiosity killed the cat,
And that the very best cheese
Is from overseas,
Now what do you think of that?
Boys, what do you think of that?

(As the last person finishes, they all laugh.)

CHARLOTTE: That was great, Dad.

CLAUDE EDWARD: Do you know any more, Jock?

*(*JOCK *looks at his watch. Everyone becomes very silent.)*

JOCK: I don't think he's going to make it.

(Lights out on KILLERS *and* YABLONSKIS*)*

WIFE: *(As before) This happened! This photo! Right here!* Smoke pouring out of your mouth. Why? Because you're smoking a cigarette? It's not that easy. Clic-clic-clic! It suggests. It insinuates. It implies. Cheese! The whole thing has got a charge. Energy! A hidden power source. A buried current which connects *what is important, what does matter!* We just got to locate it. Cheese! Clic-clic-clic! A cloud. A fog. The smoke. It's coming down. Out of your mouth. It blurs. It distorts. It's not focused. *(Screams) You're gonna blow up!!!*

(Lights out on WIFE. *Spot on* REPORTER *as he walks downstage)*

REPORTER: You understand that it's all going to happen in twenty minutes. Right? And that we still have twenty miles of hairpin curves and country roads. Right? *Right!!?* The sign there says, "Washington County, fifty-five miles per hour". But I don't know if that's there to scare or to tempt me. My fears are approaching a reckless frenzy. I'm trying to literally steer the car into the air. *But it just won't go!!*
I've thought of getting out and running but the doors are locked. So I sing, "We just aren't making it". We'll still be on the highway when the shots are fired and when the killers are making their getaway! *I will miss it! No!!!!*
I'm becoming desperate in pursuit of what can only be my own highway death. I'm focusing on distant telephone poles wondrous of which will be the instrument of pain. I'm praying only that I not live through the mutilation of part of my body. *No!!!*
Fifteen minutes to go!! And I figure we'll have to speed sixty-five miles an hour to get there.
Ten minutes to go!! And sixty-eight miles an hour! *Sixty-eight!!*
Eight minutes to go!! And we'll have to move at seventy over roads I'd feel uncomfortable going forty! No!!! No!!!!!
How can this happen? I'm getting farther and father away.

(Lights up on KILLERS *and* YABLONSKIS*)*

CHARLOTTE: *(To* JOCK, *who is looking at his watch)* Dad, couldn't we just....

JOCK: No. We've waited as long as we could. *(To* KILLERS, *shaking their hands)* Paul. Buddy. Claude Edward. It's been our pleasure.

REPORTER: Not yet. Not yet. Let's take our time, okay. *Let's take our time!!!!*

*(*KILLERS *and* YABLONSKIS *begin to exit)*

JOCK: *(With his arm around Margaret)* Don't worry.

MARGARET: I know I shouldn't. But it just meant so much to him, didn't it?

BUDDY: Do you know what I wish? I wish it were possible to make a regular date out of this. You know, like every other Saturday. I can't remember when I've had such a fun time.

REPORTER: Wait a second. Wait a sec.

PAUL: Well, there's one thing at least...

JOCK: What's that?

PAUL: The Reporter can't blame us. We tried.

(KILLERS *and* YABLONSKIS *exit. Lights out except for spot on* REPORTER)

REPORTER: *(Pleading:)* Hey, what's the.... Wait... What's the rush.... Let's just take our time... *What's the goddamn rush!!! Not yet!!! (Shouting) No!!!! Not yet!!! Wait for me!!! For Christ's sake! Wait for me!!! I'm coming!! I'm on my way!!! Wait for me!!! For me!!!!!*

(His last shout turns into a piercing scream.)

(Gun shots, off, in the direction of where the KILLERS *and* YABLONSKIS *exited.)*

(Blackout)

END OF PLAY

SCOOPING

SCOOPING was first produced by Arena Stage (Zelda Fichandler, Producing Director) opening on 4 February 1977. The cast and creative contributor were:

BUBA . . . . *Jay O Sanders*

Director . . . . *Douglas C Wager*

CHARACTER

Buba, *a reporter*

(Centerstage—a large wicker chair with a fan-shaped back faces the audience. Potted palms and ferns about and behind this wicker. Lighting throughout should be a large yellow spot on this chair.)

*(*BUBA *sits in the chair. He wears a cream-colored summer suit, straw hat, white shoes. He is in his thirties.* BUBA *speaks in two voices: Defensive voice and Aggressive voice. Throughout he speaks to himself.)*

(Stage dark)

BUBA: *(Agressive voice)* WITNESS, BUBA, WITNESS!

(Lights up. Pause)

(Defensive voice) I'm actually...yes...enjoying myself ..this...here...the attention...I'm enjoying all this interest in me...in me...it is a real...treat...a real change...an honest-to-goodness...a turn of events...being pinpointed... that is...being spotted on the charts ...name in print...caps...to finally get it out...after being such a part...yes...I am enjoying myself...to finally set the record straight... *(Aggressive)* GET IT OUT, BUBA! GET IT OUT!... *(Defensive)* I mean...actually, usually...in all humility...under normal conditions...I am the one...getting down to nitty-gritty...Buba is the one with the questions... Buba is the prober...Buba is the digger...Buba is the prime-job reporter... the top-flight scooper...that is...doing long and deep...doing down and out... inside checks...solid body punches...across the middle...in the slot...Buba is the reporter clearing away the boards...Buba the plunger with the deep penetration ...Buba with the flashy powerhouse drives...the reporter's reporter...turning corners...turning tricks...turning solid stories inside out... one on one...taking out... taking aim...taking down...lunging deep... *(Aggressive)* DAMN IT! OPEN UP, GUY! OPEN UP!... *(Defensive)* uh... as I was...this is a trip...to get it out...I was saying... quite a change... quite a turnaround...so to speak...the shoe is on the other...the tables are... to get it out...to record...and document...and headline...my story...my life and times...my playbooks...my ambitions...my personal finances...my background...my China trips...quite a new...to expose...thin...clear...expose my past...expose my magic tricks...expose my affairs...expose myself to the public...to the committee...to the judge...to the official scorer...to the drunken audience...My Story! ...My Life!... It's about time!... *(Aggressive)* LISTEN, BUBA, I WANT YOU EMPTIED, BUBA, AND EMPTIED GOOD!...OPEN UP!... *(Defensive)* I've covered a lot of news...my life...my times...no kidding... this age...in fact...blanketed a lot...smothered a lot...withered on the vine a lot...I'm full of stories...in fact...bursting with stories...at the seems...busting a gut...boy oh boy...sensational...colorful...episodes...escapades...hit and

runs...flashes...moments. I'm stuffed!...I'm stuffed!...me!...my story!...my
life!... *(Aggressive)* OPEN!...

(Defensive) in one...one story...is this the kind of stuff you want...will it play...
good copy...hold attention...sell papers...in one story...will this be cut up...
my quotes out of context...set down straight...kept clean...out of the hands
of children...babes...in one story...you will love this...I wear white shoes...
am I enunciating...is the tape running...football...a bowl game...white shoes
my trademark...familiar...up to par...need I say more...fans in the stands
hold up cards which spell out my name...Booster Club...crowd noise...band
plays Dixie...drush on a baton twirler...there's a story in that...I roll back...get
the picture...with the ball...pigskin...rolling back... before the game outside
my house...I'm carried on shoulders onto the team bus...bonfires...there's
a story in that...I roll back...fast on my feet...white shoes...just sports-page
stuff...what about a front page teaser...third quarter...is this the kind of stuff
you'll print...I'm rolling...ra-ra-ra-ra...out of the pocket...arm cocked...
ra-ra-ra-ra, surveying downfield...ra-ra-ra-ra...then blind-side hit...hit...
a hit...my knees...pop...white shoes...white shoes...I WAS A BETTER
QUARTERBACK THAN WILLIE JOE NAMATH BEFORE THAT
HAPPENED!... AND I WAS A BETTER BASEBALL PLAYER THAN
CANIGLIARO BEFORE I GOT HIT IN THE EYE...AND I WAS A BETTER
GOLFER THAN CHAMPAGNE TONY BEFORE I DIED IN THAT PLANE
CRASH...my story...see...my spotlight...my headline...my fame...AND
WHILE I'M AT IT...WHILE I'M SETTING THE FUCKING RECORD
BOOKS STRAIGHT...I JUST WANT IT KNOWN...OUT IN THE CLEAR...
SEE, OVER THE NEWS WIRES...TAP IT OUT...YOU UNDERSTAND...
THAT I WAS A BETTER ACTOR THAN BURTON BEFORE I MET LIZ...A
BETTER CANDIDATE THAN MUSKIE BEFORE I CRIED IN THE SNOW...
A BETTER JUDGE THAN DOUGLAS BEFORE MY STROKE...BETTER
SONGMAN THAN DYLAN BEFORE I GOT MY BIKE...AND...AND...A
GOOD SIGHT...A MUCH BETTER...A LOT BIGGER...KILLER-MAN THAN
MANSON EVER HOPED TO BE...EVER DREAMED OF BEING...BEFORE
I GOT PUT AWAY!!! *(Pause)* ... *(Aggressive)* Now, Buba...now listen, guy...
pay good attention...get my drift...take my lead...I want you exposed thin...
I want your heart to pour...your psyche to drain like it has never been
drained before...I want your life story out...IN DETAIL, DAMN IT!...
(Defensive) My story goes...it goes like...I'm stuffed...I'm full... In fact...
it goes like...like nothing else...that's come before...it's an original...it's an
eye-catcher...it's wet ink...my story goes...it feels so great to get this off my
chest!...off my mind!...off my record!... *(Aggressive)* I want the rights to
your body...the deed to your dreams... I want it all put on the line...on the
chopping block...on the money...thrown on the run...on the lamb...off your
shoulder...out of your mind...TELL ME...TELL ME...YOUR TWO-FISTED
CONNECTION TO THE OUTSIDE...THE FRONT PAGE...THE DREAM
OF DREAMS...TELL ME...I WANT IT OUT IN THE OPEN.... I WANT AN
OUTPOUR THAT CANNOT BE STOPPED!... *(Defensive)* it goes like...like

this little ditty...or the time...the time when...this one's better...much, much better...oh it is...oh it is...it'll grab...hold you...spellbind...get inside you...stick to the wall...this one...I'm in the apartment...let's get this down...with my fiance...for bed...dressed...music...Eric Satie...white wine...as it was...drifting... comfortable...oh so drifting...and lazy...and lounging...when...when in fact... let's get this straight...and true to form...when...the doorbell...no alarm...no thought...why not...without concern then...boy, have times changed...boy oh boy...my life...my fiancée is at the door...since then...if it's a friend, don't invite him in...as it was...a car is broken down...down the way...down the road...a flat...two women need a phone...I hope they're not going to wait here...no kidding...she unlocks the door...I'm swimming...without interest... in my thoughts...without interest...without...empty...white wine...three men erupt...ski masks...erupt...so to speak...what the hell is this...what the...this is true...a shotgun...boy oh boy...black army boots...fuck the army...fuck the pigs...they burst in...a blind terror...door splinters...you are intruding...just like that...like animals...what the...no reason for this...no sense...senseless... without...I'm stuffed...she screams...

(He screams.)

...I won't panic...hold the line...ra-ra-ra-ra...dig in...dig in...every dog has his...what...his stalking ground...a man's home is...you are stepping on the lines...my space...the boundaries...this is my lot...my life...my story... my claim...my ball and field...a terror let loose...belted to the floor...hot... coughing...kick...they are exploding me...she is gagged...boy oh boy...where are you taking her...a blurr...a kick...kick...PATTY!...PATTY!...but that's JUST ONE...JUST ONE...in another...I told you I'm crammed full...the next...the next course...I'm at the sixth game...Fenway Park...didn't you believe me... I'm on the stump in New Hampshire...I'm on the stage at the Stardust... I'm a communist...I'm a hypocrite...I'm a dreamboat...I'm disguised as an elevator operator so I can get an exclusive with the star...I'm roving where stories are made...packaged...sealed...arranged neatly on the shelf...where pennants are lost...where battlelines are drawn...where elections are fixed... where masterpieces are uncovered...where mercenaries are bought and paid for...where the guilty verdict rings out loud and clear...as do the innocent screams... *(He screams.)* ...I am roving...yes...low to the ground...nose to the grindstone...scooping up stories...tips...hot leads...arm cocked...and shoving them into my pockets...shoveling them into my mouth...stuffing them into my belly...into my brain...folding them into my envelope...pressing them into my book...into my life...my life and times...I'm full!...I'm bloated!... TAKE ME...SCOOP ME...OPEN UP MY GUT AND CLEAN ME OUT... IT'S MY TURN...IT'S GOTTA BE MY TURN...MY TIME...MY MOMENT... MY LIFE STORY!...

(Long pause)

(Aggressive) Hey there, Buba...hey there guy...I'm your...we were in the war together...on double dates together...I'm your best friend, pal...bosom buddy...so why don't...our fathers grew up together...I've got your best interests at heart...why don't you just...I'm concerned about your future... I want to help...listen...console...congratulate you for winning the race...so why don't you just open...I want to be the first to shake your hand...to get you out of a jam...open up for your ol' buddy...to speak up for your side... I want to buy you a drink...get you a job...dance at your wedding...cheer you on...ra-ra-ra-ra...so why don't you just release and...put yourself in these hands...my hands...a pal's...true-blue...and drift and...into my thoughts and... into my dreams and...release and...open, friend...open... *(Defensive)* uh...uh... SCOOP ME, BUBA!!...*(Aggressive)* I've come from all around...to sit at your table...to hear you out...to be your best man...from great plains...big skys... crowded squares...from where the Yankees play...and the Rams...and Celtics...from sidewalks and boardrooms and shop windows...from the inside of stuffy movie houses...and from mass parades...from where it is still safe to walk down the streets...and from the monuments of peace...to here... to you...my pal...I've come...so why don't...I mean...let me put it...clear away the fences...the debris...the wreckage and waste...this way...why don't you just...the stone walls...and the body guards...why don't you... *(Defensive)* OPEN ME...CLEANSE ME...RA-RA-RA-RA...GET YOUR HOOKS IN AND DIG ME OUT!!... *(Aggressive)* whatever is in you...interests me...yes... whatever you see...my eyes wish to see...whatever in part has struck you as odd...as desirous...as eventful...demeaning...whatever you wish to discuss... me too...so do I...whatever town...hamlet... living room...chair...you call home...me too...whatever makes you relax...drowsy...drift...oh so drift... and the same for tastes...hates...morals...innermost fears...we share it all... we share words and meanings behind words...gestures which neither of us ever knew we had...we share a walking style...a speech pattern...a won-loss record...a bodily rhythm...we share a table in a crowded restaurant...we share a common ground.... *(Defensive)* PLACE ME...LABEL ME...MAGNIFY ME...PIN ME DOWN AND TICKET ME...SCOOP...BUBA SCOOP!... *(Aggressive)* if you stand before an opening day crowd...I stand...simple... fact...if you want only what is simple in life...the basics...the bottom line of pleasure...I want...fact...you walk along the beach at sunset...those are my footprints in the sand...you take a drive through the mountains...where do you think I am...fact...you face the mugger...you talk at length about social injustice...you see your fortune in the cards...you cheer on Hank Aaron...you dare to walk under ladders...you disperse the mob...you refuse to cooperate with the committee...you wait for the meteor to hit...WELL SO DO I, PAL... SO DO IT...GOD DAMN IT, BUBA, DO IT!...GET IT OUT!!!

(Defensive) IN ANOTHER ONE...I was where...I was what...I am with... in another...with angle...with twist...with story...with another ACTION -PACKED MOMENT OUT OF MY LIFE!...MY STORY!...*(Aggressive)* I SAID, GET IT OUT!...*(Defensive)* Explosions...I hear them...yes...I race...get this...

I am running down a wooden dock...behind me...gun shots...closer...
CLOSER...get this...hundreds of yellows...behind...fling...push and shove...
into the sea...running down a wooden dock...to an American ship...fire
erupts...so to speak...bombers...helicopters overhead...buzz...get this...to a
ship crowded with refugees...REFUGEES!!...*(Aggressive)* You can't squirm
out of my grasp...you can't block my drive...stop my plunge... check my
run...better not even try...'CAUSE I AIN'T NO SMALL TIME AUTOGRAPH
HOUND!!... *(Defensive)* Panic...I see it...mothers' cries...the wooden dock...
the world on fire...when a butt of a gun...an M-l...knocked down...behind
me...I see it...thousands of yellow peasants...DOOMSDAY...DOOMSDAY...
it's all come to a head...I stand...running down...isn't this incredible...the
boat begins to clear...the wooden dock...I see it...clears itself away...bodies
splash...push and shove...I am running down a wooden dock...trying to
escape...A REFUGEE...A PRIME TIME REFUGEE!!...but that's just one...
JUST ONE!... *(Aggressive)* I'm gonna take you out so fast...gonna fuckin'
burn rubber across your face...gonna dance you by the scruff of your neck...
gonna release such a psychic assault, fella...I'm gonna POUND MY STAKES
AND LAY GOOD CLAIM...I WANT YOUR STORY!!... *(Defensive)* in
another...in focus...I see myself...strapped to a chair...a corduroy hood...
I can't see it...corduroy...write that down...isn't that odd...to a chair...I'm
drifting...oh so drifting...boy, have times changed...boy oh boy...stuck in a
chair...stuck in a warehouse...stuck in Utah...I see myself...arm cocked...M-l
cocked...ra-ra-ra-ra...SO LET'S DO IT...bang-bang-bang-bang...I'm crazy...
I'm a dingbat...there's a story in that...I'm a murderer...I'm a newsmaker...
there's a story in that bang-bang-bang-bang...I'M CRAMMED FULL I TELL
YOU...SCOOP!!!... *(Aggressive)* I'm gonna show your weaknesses...your
soft spots...your bad acts and spills... I will penetrate your thoughts like a
burrowing screw...YOU CANNOT JUST PLUCK ME OUT...I will hang out
your dirty sheets...and I will pick through your policies...your platforms...
your friends...your garbage...your ten-year-old speeches...I will parade
before you...your mistresses...and your gallbladder scars...I will show your
bathroom deals...and freebie junkets...your electro-shock treatments...and
underworld connections...your "heal the wounds" speeches...and your
assassination plots?... *(Defensive)* I see myself...in pinstripes...in magazines...
on wanted posters...I see my face before millions...before and after...before
the defeat and the victory...before the picture is snapped...I see my face
done in fireworks...in marble...in greasepaint...in sweat... *(Aggressive)* I will
present you dressed for dinner...dressed for golf...dressed like an idiot in
shoes that look like boats...I will record you strolling...ranting...smiling...
crying in two feet of snow...I will show you exuding love of God...love
of self...love of children...love of golden retrievers...love of the poor and
afflicted...I will show you in the raw as no man has ever been shown in the
raw before...as naked...empty...solitary...on the cliff...blind...and screaming...

(He screams.)

(Defensive) I hear my voice getting weaker...lost in static...I hear myself cheering...cajoling...whispering...I hear the rhythmic calypso of my voice... and the acid rock of my voice...and the squeaks in my voice...I hear myself chanting insults...orders...mantras...my voice calling to me from the night... from the other side of the moon...from the other side of the grave...from the other side of the room...my voice holding its own in debate...in the marketplace...in the stadium...in the hot seat...my voice amplified...and muffled...faceless...and speechless...I see myself as I would like to be seen... as I am seen...as I will be seen...I see myself on a film taken in a bank...I see my face up in lights...I see my name on the back of leather jackets...my name on the ticket...on the ballot...on the credits...on the check...I SEE THE EPISODES OF MY LIFE...THE MOMENTOUS TIMES OF MY LIFE...THE NEWSWORTHY EVENTS OF MY LIFE...I SEE THE SPECIALS AND THE RERUNS!!. SCOOP ME, BUBA, SCOOP ME!... *(Aggressive)* I WILL SHOW YOU IN PAIN!...pain forever...pain unfulfilled...pain remorseless... vindictive...wanton...and aggressive pain that will rip the walls out of your chest...I will show you frothing...slashing...bitter and defeated...the sadness of the world on your face...I will get under your skin...under your fingernails...under your makeshift walls of defense...AND I WILL THRASH...BEAT...BEAT UNTIL YOU HAVE OPENED UP...LET ME IN...until you have cleaned the air...until you have WITNESSED!!...OPEN UP AND WITNESS!...I will break you with tortures untried...unheard of...unimagined...I will dig my hand into your chest AND DRAW YOU OUT SCREAMING... *(He screams)* ...WITNESS!...like it or not...like me or not...no stopping me...no roadblocks...no bulletproof Caddies...no press secretaries...no fake treaties...no palace guards...no new amendments. WITNESS!...there is nothing that can block my path...get me out of your hair...off your back...don't even try...because it is too late for that... WITNESS!?...nothing that will soften me...tempt me...bribe me...weaken my drive...dilute my effort...call me out looking...stroke my ego...NOTHING!... SO YOU MIGHT AS WELL...JUST AS WELL...JUST OPEN UP, BUBA... OPEN UP AND SWEEP IT OUT...LET IT POUR...DRAIN...LET IT POUR... AND WITNESS, BUBA, WITNESS...WITNESS!!!

(Long pause)

(Defensive) I'm actually...this...enjoying myself...immensely...being the focus of...of all this...getting my story out...on the line...on the money...being spotted on the charts...I must...I must say...it's real...an honest-to-goodness... a turn of events...uh...*(Lights begin to fade out)*...to finally...I mean...after being such a part...of things...so filled...bursting at the seems...after...to finally...the attention...the spotlight...set the fucking record books straight...at last...at long last...it's now my turn...my time...get it off my chest...my picture in the paper...my story...my story...my voice...

(Blackout)

BROADWAY PLAY PUBLISHING INC PLAYWRIGHTS' COLLECTIONS

PLAYS BY ALAN BOWNE
BEIRUT
FORTY-DEUCE
SHARON AND BILLY

PLAYS BY LONNIE CARTER
LEMUEL
GULLIVER
GULLIVER REDUX

PLAYS BY STEVE CARTER
DAME LORRAINE
HOUSE OF SHADOWS
MIRAGE
ONE LAST LOOK
TEA ON INAUGURATION DAY

PLAYS BY ANTHONY CLARVOE
LET'S PLAY TWO
THE LIVING
SHOW AND TELL

PLAYS BY DONALD FREED
ALFRED AND VICTORIA: A LIFE
CHILD OF LUCK
IS HE STILL DEAD?

PLAYS BY ALLAN HAVIS
HOSPITALITY
MINK SONATA
MOROCCO

PLAYS BY ALLAN HAVIS, VOLUME TWO
A DARING BRIDE
THE LADIES OF FISHER COVE
SAINTE SIMONE

PLAYS BY TONY KUSHNER
A BRIGHT ROOM CALLED DAY
THE ILLUSION

PLAYS BY LOUIS PHILLIPS
BONE THE SPEED
CARWASH
CONRAD ON THE VINE
ETHIOPIA
THE MAN WHO ATE EINSTEIN'S BRAIN
PRECISION MACHINES

PLAYS BY AISHAH RAHMAN
THE MOJO AND THE SAYSO
ONLY IN AMERICA
UNFINISHED WOMEN CRY IN NO MAN'S LAND WHILE A BIRD DIES
IN A GILDED CAGE

PLAYS BY EDWIN SÁNCHEZ
CLEAN
FLOOR SHOW: DOÑA SOL AND HER TRAINED DOG
TRAFFICKING IN BROKEN HEARTS

PLAYS BY NAOMI WALLACE
IN THE HEART OF AMERICA
SLAUGHTER CITY
THE WAR BOYS